Life, Life

Thy life's a miracle. Speak yet again.

King Lear IV, vi, 55.

DON CUPITT

Life, Life

Published in 2003 by Polebridge Press, P.O. Box 6144, Santa Rosa, California 95406.

ISBN 0-944344-96-8

Library of Congress Cataloging-in-Publication Data

Cupitt, Don.
  Life, Life / Don Cupitt
    p. cm.
  Includes bibliographical references (p.) and index.
  ISBN 0-944344-96-8
    1. Life. 2. Life–Religious aspects–Christianity. I. Title.

  BD431.C96 2003
  128–dc21

                               2003049896

Cover photograph by Maurice Jassak. Image provided by www.seevancouverbc.com. Used by permission.

for Sebastian, aged 7, who
asked how he could get
into this book

Contents

Introduction

Ordinary people are said to expect philosophy to be about the Meaning of Life. What, they ask, is the point of it all?

In this book I am going as far as possible towards directly answering these questions. Much of the time I'm starting from the uses and the meaning of the word 'life', and trying to keep very close to the thought of ordinary people. I quote standard idioms from ordinary language, and print them in **boldface Roman** type.

Nothing guarantees in advance that everything in life can be assimilated into one great system of thought, so this book is inevitably unsystematic. It's written in short sections, the idea being that you'll read them in ones and twos, at odd moments, until you have built up an impression of the endless range and wonder of the modern idea of life.

You will remember that Lewis Carroll presents *The Hunting of the Snark* in fits, a 'fit' being a section of a poem as well as a short, violent, compressed episode. I actually wrote this book with the working title *Life: A Fragmentary Philosophy in Forty Fits*, but it was obvious that I couldn't get away with such a title.

To understand the book, you will need to become more aware of ordinary language, and of what is currently happening in it. Get into the habit of looking out for the three or four hundred most common and vivid life-idioms, and you will gradually begin to see how the whole of our worldview, our religion, and our morality are currently being reorganized around the idea of life. Several professional authors have told me that they, too, have noticed what is happening; others may find that the full revelation takes time and a good deal of attention to words. The new religion of life is simply of *this* life. Deep down that's what we already think; but it is only slowly coming to the surface and becoming explicit.

Cambridge, 2002–2003 D.C.

Life Is Everything

Life is everything. Life is God.
Leo Tolstoy, *War and Peace*

Life is like nothing, because it is everything.
William Golding, *Free Fall*

In the year 2002 the old Queen Mother died in London at the age of 101. There had been abundant time to prepare for this event, and the Palace could not fail to remember that when Diana, Princess of Wales had died, the public had been affronted by the way the Royal Family had at that time retreated into privacy and silence, as if declining to have any part in the general grief. That mistake must not be made again, so on this occasion both the Queen herself and Prince Charles recorded short statements, about two and four minutes long respectively, for television.

These statements were intended to relate the private grief of the Family to the public mourning of the nation, and to set the completed life of an individual against the larger background of the ongoing national life. More than that, it was also — as always — the sort of occasion on which everyone feels a need to invoke a universal, cosmic background to our existence. Given the special status of the Queen and her Heir in relation to the national church, and the Queen's own professed personal faith, there was every reason to expect some use of religious language.

As it turned out, however, neither statement made any mention of the soul, the world, God, faith, religion, sin, judgement, or life after death. The traditional religious vocabulary was entirely lacking; instead,

1

both statements made repeated use of the word 'life'. Prince Charles, who used the word five or six times, is not known to be a student of philosophy, but two of his uses of 'life' had markedly Nietzschean overtones.

It cannot be doubted that advisers checked both statements very carefully to make certain that they expressed only the most unexceptionable sentiments in the most generally intelligible language. Here then, I suggest, we have an illustration of the striking fact that in the past few decades *life* has become our most popular totalizing word – by which I mean, the word we use when we want to talk about 'it all' or 'everything' – and various 'life' idioms have become the dominant form of religious language that is usable in public.[1]

I first recognized this in about 1997, when I was casting about for a new way of writing philosophy and theology for a public that seemed to have become highly resistant to both subjects. I thought of an indirect approach: instead of vainly attempting to interest the public in my own ideas, I would find a convincing empirical method of demonstrating what philosophical and religious beliefs the general public already hold. I would do this by collecting all I could of the stock phrases current in everyday speech in which people choose to articulate their own thoughts about **the meaning of life**.[2] Just as the man in Molière's play was astounded to discover that he'd been speaking prose all his life, so the ordinary English-speaking person would be convicted out of her own mouth of already having created a philosophical and religious outlook, whether she recognized it or not.

I sat around with a notepad, looking dreamy and jotting down phrases. In time I also purchased a shelf of dictionaries – of slang, of idioms, of proverbs, of quotations and so on. But I still possess the very first sheet of notes I made. At some later date, perhaps in 1998, I went over this sheet with a highlighter pen, marking the terms which occur most frequently. They are 'life' and 'it all', both of which are found six times. It was these two terms that stood out and continued to do so, so that in due course they became the topics of the two 'Everyday Speech' books of 1999, *The New Religion of Life in Everyday Speech* and *The Meaning of It All in Everyday Speech* (both London: SCM Press). These books aimed to turn the tables on my critical reviewers. I would look innocent and say: 'I'm not trying to press *my* ideas upon *you*. Heaven forbid! No, I'm showing you what a deep and interesting thinker you already are: I'm pointing out the implications of the language that *you yourself* are already using'.

Now, if my critics and all those ordinary people chose to be smart and suspicious, they could require me to justify my singling out from everyday speech stock phrases that incorporate terms like 'life' and 'it all' as being of special philosophical and religious interest. Why not focus the enquiry around other terms such as 'believe', 'absolute' and 'certain'? The best answer is surely that people in general evidently find that 'life' and 'it all' are our best totalizing terms: that is, when we talk of life we invoke everything about the human condition, human experience, and human knowledge as it appears to us humans who cannot but see everything from the point of view of living beings with an intense *interest* in life. The word 'life' comprehensively reminds us of what we are and from what angle we see everything – 'it all.' And in fact I found that the new 'life' idioms and 'it all' idioms are remarkably numerous. It seems that in modern times we have become acutely aware that life is everything, that life is all we have and all we will ever have, and that our being in life flavours and shapes the way we see everything. In the past, thinkers have constructed God-centred, Being-centred and Knowledge-centred visions of everything; but today it seems that the life-centred point of view serves us best. It leaves nothing out: as Wittgenstein says, 'The world and life are one'.[3]

Very well: but why has the old religious vocabulary so suddenly gone out of use, and why have the new terms so suddenly come to seem much more appropriate? Why the big changeover?

The historical story that I have already told elsewhere remains, I believe, substantially correct. It invokes 'the discovery of time', 'the discovery of the mind', the discovery of *bildung* (the development of the personality during one's formative years), and the discovery of the innocence of everyday modern life, all in the period around 1780-1870.[4] After the French Revolution a new commercial and industrial civilization led by the middle classes began to develop very rapidly. Its outlook was and is highly urban and 'historical' – which means progressive, humanistic, liberal and democratic. People had begun to understand that history is made by human beings, and that it involves real and deep change. Through the Romantic movement and the rise of psychology, a strong interest in individual human subjectivity and individual life experience also began to develop. People began to see the human life world as being the primary world in which we all live, and the novel became the dominant literary form. Naturally enough, novelists began to show a special interest in the major events of the human **life cycle**. Everyone became highly conscious of the story of her own life, and especially of the for-

mation and development of the personality through childhood and ado-
lescence to adulthood, courtship and marriage. Not least through the
novel, women began to emerge into equality, both in art and in social
and public life. And finally, people cast aside their traditional moral ani-
mus against big cities and began to affirm the innocence of secular urban
everydayness. *Plein air* impressionists painting Paris are a world away
from Hogarth's doomed and stinking London. Even a figure as intensely
religious as Vincent Van Gogh sees very clearly that modern city life
escapes traditional religious censure. The 'City of Man' cannot *simply* be
seen as an image of Hell. In particular, the modern city escapes the old
distinction between the sacred and the secular, or profane. The two have
become fused together in a new outlook which dramatically revalues
everything that is 'human' – that is, finite, temporal, contingent, and of
this world.

Two of the very best statements of the new outlook are
Wordsworth's straightforward confidence in the innocence of bodily life
and sensuous experience, and Tolstoy's affirmation written in the late
1860s – ascribed to Pierre towards the end of *War and Peace*: 'Life is God',
and 'To love life is to love God'.[5]

Thus by 1870 or so, in the work of certain major artists, life is emerging as the new religious object. It is within us, it is that in which we live
and move and have our being, and it is also in a sense over against us.
My life is my own personal span, and I have to decide **what I want to
do with my life**. At the same time, life is also our other, our milieu and
our only home. It may be personified as calling for our commitment to
it, as guiding us, as teaching us lessons and as dealing out to us our fates.
Ordinary people's outlook has gradually become more and more life-
centred, until by today people instinctively take a life-centred view even
of death itself. Thus the funeral service has become **A Thanksgiving for
the life of...** and the memorial service is **A Celebration of the life of**
the dead person. Increasingly, even the churches are opening woodland
burial grounds where corpses, instead of lying 'asleep' waiting for the
General Resurrection, are consigned to be recycled into the biological
life of this world.

So we see today that a long process of return to this world, to time,
the body, and everyday life – a process that perhaps, began with or
shortly before the Protestant Reformation – has been largely realized.
Early Protestant attitudes to the senses, the body, and everyday life were
decidedly mixed. On the one hand there was a desire to assert the holiness of everyday work and especially of domestic life, a theme to which

seventeenth-century Dutch painting bears eloquent witness; but on the other hand there was also a pessimistic conviction that sin could not be finally conquered and the human condition could not be greatly improved by anything short of the return of Christ. In the nineteenth century that mixture of optimistic and pessimistic strains continues, as we are reminded when we note that Tolstoy's Pierre, who so extravagantly praises life, is also a prisoner of war who has recently lost his faith and has been having a cruelly hard time – and that the Paris whose everyday life is so eloquently hymned by a long line of painters had just gone through the horrors of the Franco-Prussian War. Claude Monet himself had experienced great hardship and had left the city – but here he is back home, and Paris is *paradis* again.

In the twentieth century the same ambivalence continues, as Henri Matisse maintains the vision of this life as Edenic whilst living under the Vichy government in southern France. But modern people take a non-realist view of life. It is not an iron cage. Our **life is what we make it.** By changing the way ordinary people see themselves and their world, and by changing the political and economic arrangements under which they live, we can make everyday life paradisal. It can be done. It's up to us. There is therefore no excuse for *not* adopting, and battling to realize, the Edenic vision.

So it has come to pass that since the 1960s the new religion of ordinary life that Tolstoy had adumbrated a century earlier is now the effective religion of ordinary people, embodied in all the stock phrases about life that are common currency. **All life is sacred**, and we must **have faith in life**. We all of us want to **love life**, to **live life to the full,** to **trust it**, to **commit ourselves to it**, and to **make the most of it while it lasts**. Two centuries ago, Hegel described the process by which the entire supernatural order returns into this world, coming down to earth and being diffused through the common life of ordinary people. We should not *regret* this process; its happening is part of the working-out of Christianity's own logic. After Protestantism, the next step is the religion of ordinary life. As I have suggested elsewhere, the traditional 'church' sort of Christianity should not grumble about this, but should rather rejoice to see itself as at last being elbowed aside *by its own fulfilment*. Like John the Baptist, it should graciously give place to its own proper heir and successor.

I said all this in my little book, *The New Religion of Life in Everyday Speech* (1999) and its two successors. But I made some mistakes. I concentrated the argument around an attempt to demonstrate that life has become the new religious object, trying to show in some detail how the various things that we used to say about God have now been reshaped into sayings about life. We need to **have faith in life**, we **should not tempt life**, because **nobody is bigger than life**, and so on. This 'interest' or *tendenz* of the argument led me to stress the respects in which life resembles God, and relatively to neglect the various important ways in which life is quite different from God. The result was a little book that was accurate so far as it went, but which failed to realize fully the good idea from which it had begun.

There are two ways in which life differs markedly from God. They arise from the fact that the 'omni' attributes of God come out quite differently from those of life, because God is (or was) transcendent, simple, unmixed perfection, and sovereign over all things; whereas life is finite, temporal, immanent and all-inclusive. God is pure holiness and goodness, whereas life is baggy and shapeless, and includes all the opposites – bliss and wretchedness, comedy and tragedy, fullness and emptiness, good and ill, holiness and profanity, all bundled together in one great package. The result is that saying 'Yes' to life is markedly different from saying 'Yes' to God. When we say 'Yes' to life we say 'Amen' to *all* of it as a package deal, and thereafter the so-called Problem of Evil does not arise. We are required to renounce the victim psychology and the old impulse to complain about being unfairly treated.

Those who say 'Yes' to God, on the other hand, take sides. They commit themselves to a dualistic view of life, at every point choosing this and rejecting *that*. Inevitably, they have great difficulties with suffering and evil – not least because with our historical picture of nature it has become very hard to maintain that aggressiveness and death are no more than secondary intruders into a life world that was originally designed to work best without them. But there it is: those who love life say 'Yes' to it all and try to learn never to complain, whereas those who love God pick and choose in the hope that they will one day be spectacularly vindicated.

The second way in which life differs from God is that – unless they claim to believe in a 'life force', or something of the kind – the lovers of life are non-realists. Life is not a great Being, self-existent and utterly distinct from us. Life is just the going on of things in the human life world. Life is our human traffic, our business, our conversation. Life is communication: life is our world, and life is what we make it. A religion of commitment to life is therefore the only fully immediate and non-dualistic religion, for it refuses to make any distinction between our outer life and our inner life, or between secular and sacred spheres of life, or between loving God and loving **it all** or loving one's neighbour. Nor does it distinguish between temporal and eternal concerns: on the contrary, it simply calls for an unhesitating and unreserved ethical response to **the call of life** — where you are and *Right Now* — i.e. the sort of response that the teacher Jesus of Nazareth is reported to have demanded. Life is chaotic: we can't expect to be able to totalize it speculatively. But by the way we commit ourselves ethically to life and to our neighbour we can *make sense* of it. I say again: our ethical commitment to life is that which alone injects moral intelligibility into life.

Here we should notice that the religion of life is metaphysically very different from traditional theism. In the religious outlook in which we were all brought, up there were two great totalizing ideas: God and the finite or 'created' order which is usually called 'the World'. I am now replacing those two with a single new object, which may be called Being or life. It is finite, temporal and contingent. Above all, it is a single, immanent, continuous whole of which we are seamlessly part. It is outsideless. Life is, simply, everything.

Chapter 2

From the Cosmos to Life

How can we best describe the milieu which encompasses us, the medium in which we live immersed, the Other or the Not-Self, the place or context in which we find our existence to have been set? What is this all about me in which I'm me, and in which I live and move and have my being? It is extraordinarily difficult to find the right vocabulary with which even to formulate the question here, but at least we can be clear about two of the most important answers to it.

A few centuries ago, under the influence of religious doctrine, we thought of the milieu around us in which our existence is set as **the created world**, **Nature**, or **the Cosmos**. It was a stage or a home purposely built for us to occupy, with a built-in framework of physical and moral law. We had been made for it, and then popped into it. Pantheists might speak of it as God, and others might refer to it as **the Whole** or **it all**; but the most neutral expression is probably **the world** or even (nowadays) **the Universe**.[1]

Today it seems that we have ceased, or are ceasing, to think of our setting as being a ready-made home, specially designed for us. We are also ceasing to think of ourselves as having been specially created —and certainly not as having been at first specially created *as adults*, independently made and then inserted into the world. On the contrary, when we examine our situation from our specifically human point of view, we see that our self-perception and our perception of the world have from the outset evolved together and in parallel. We've always been deeply interwoven with our matrix, the two of us rather like reflections of each other. So the Other, or the milieu in which our existence is set, or out of which we have gradually managed to differentiate ourselves, is nowadays best described as *life*. We usually think of ourselves as *immanent* in life – life being like an envelope around us, in and through which we see everything.[1]

The Other, then, used to be the visible Creation, Nature, the Cosmos, the ready-made world out there into which we have been put. It was a more-or-less unchanging stage on which the drama of our human life would be played out from the beginning to the end of history. But today the primary Other is Life – life biological, social and cultural; life as a complex, surging, ongoing process of exchange; life as the going on of things in the human world. Life as a buzz of communication, like the glorious sound – a surging roar of chirruping insects – that rises from a Basque meadow on a summer evening.

So the matrix, or the milieu, used to be the world, but now it is life – for many or most people, at least. This makes a huge difference to the way we see the human situation. For example, *world people* think more in terms of space and knowledge, whereas *life people* think more in terms of time, human relationships, and stories. World people set out systematically to survey the environment, classifying and tabulating its contents and seeing what usable resources it offers for humans to exploit. They are like Victorian pioneers – keen on science and engineering, on maps and trade, and on developing infrastructure. They seek efficiently to exploit the resources available, in order to optimize general human well-being. They are very keen on our science-based industrial civilization: they believe in research and development, and in technical progress.

By contrast, life people see the human world as a theatre. They scarcely notice the physical environment, because they are so absorbed by the varied ways in which people interact with each other and construct the stories of their lives. They love myth, drama, and fiction. They are intensely interested in the very mysterious and difficult questions of what *action* is in the interpersonal realm, and of what produces human happiness.

Life people and world people differ very interestingly on the question of knowledge. World people by and large still maintain the old insistence that we can act effectively only on the basis of a good empirical knowledge of how things are in the empirical world around us. More than that: like the people of the Enlightenment, they propose we should set out to take a full inventory. We should describe, classify, and tabulate the whole lot. Furthermore, if we seek control over at least part of the environment, we need to do more than just describe it in full; we must theorize its workings. We need not just natural history, but scientific theory and research – and then some detailed cost analyses.

World people then see us as being set in a ready-made, ready-ordered physical world, which must be studied closely if we are to act effectively. For life people, by contrast, knowledge and the physical world are relatively unimportant. Consider how rarely Shakespeare's characters pay close attention to their physical environment, and how unthinkable it is that any of them should actually be engaged in *research* – a word that had scarcely been invented in Shakespeare's day. His people are completely absorbed in their relationships and in the shaping of their own lives. Knowledge is not important to them, but they do watch plays and they do know a lot of stories. They live very intensely in and by their self-expression. In fact they talk non-stop.

World people, we gather, are realists: for them, there is a real world out there with an objective intelligible order. We need to learn about it to live successfully in it, and are able to do so because of our interesting dual nature: on the one hand we are ourselves physical objects and indeed animals in the world – which is why we *need* to pay such close attention to our environment – but on the other hand we also possess a unique quality: a contemplative rational nature that makes us capable of language, of enquiry and of theoretical knowledge. One half of us is a part of the world, and the other half stands back a little in order to observe it and think things out.

Life people are non-realists. They are not interested in the idea of an intelligible, real, nonhuman 'it' world. They are like teenagers or young adults, wholly caught up in the endless streaming process of symbolic exchange which is life, and the complex dance of human meanings, feelings and valuations. Notice that in the human life world everything is coded into language, everything is linguistically mediated. Life people are not too much bothered about any alleged world of extralinguistic fact. They don't need knowledge: for them, living is not a matter of applied *knowledge* but rather of applied *stories*. For greater success in living they'd like to have more poetical power, and a bigger lexicon of good stories for building their lives with. To them it is obvious that art and religion are much bigger influences upon our behaviour than science is.

Now I have been suggesting that especially since the work of such figures as Darwin, Nietzsche and Freud we have been gradually shifting our basic common philosophy. Instead of imagining ourselves as special creatures set by God in a world, a cosmos, we increasingly perceive ourselves as purely *immanent* beings, immersed in *life*. And we are beginning to glimpse the magnitude of the philosophical shift that this involves.[2]

Life, however, is non-realist. Life is not a great ready-made thing out there. Life is ourselves, life is what we make it, life is a buzz that we generate around ourselves, especially in the heart of big cities. Life is the ceaseless whirling dance of signs in which we are caught up, Nicolas Poussin's *Dance to the Music of Time*.[3]

Life Is Contingent

In the world of everyday life – which, I am insisting, is the world of ordinary language, the primary world, the one into which we were first inducted and in which we continue to live – everything is contingent. We are well aware that we can recognize some events as being meant by other people, and some pressures and 'necessities' as having been imposed upon us by other people. But we do not experience *everything* as being in some way meant or necessitated to happen. On the contrary, in the life world everything just happens to happen, or turn out, or befall in the way it does. When we speak of 'befalling' here, the fall in question was no doubt originally the fall of a die; and similarly, when we speak about the way things 'pan out', the panning in question was originally the panning of a hopeful prospector in the goldfields of Northern California. In such circumstances people may desperately want to believe in luck or fate, and may look very hard for some way of improving their chances. But the way we use the metaphors, and such other expressions as 'the run of the balls', 'the luck of the draw' and 'the lap of the gods', shows that in the end we know that everything is the product of time and chance: everything just happens. Too much looking for meaning or 'meant-ness' is a waste of time.

That everything in the life world is contingent becomes obvious when we pause to consider how it must originally have come into being. Emerging from their animal background into the first glimmerings of consciousness some tens of thousands of years ago, early humans started with little but their own intense sociability and their need to develop a common language – which in effect means a common world to co-inhabit. The world of sense-experience available to them was very various, chaotic and fast-changing. How could a common world be built out of it? Briefly, they had to use language to make bits of their sense-experience differentiated, clarified and *common*. They had to find out by trial and error which bits of sense-experience could be referred out into objectivity, fixed and stabilized as parts of a common world. It was not an easy thing to do: even to this day we are often not quite sure what's out there and what's only in our sense organs. The main point is that we have to learn to do the referring out in a standard, rule-governed way. In the end we succeeded and it was all done, just by the talk of us human beings. So the life world evolved: we all live in it, and for the most part it works very well. But it follows from this account of how the life world came into being that everything in it is contingent, and the order we seem to see in it is merely an order that we ourselves have imputed to it. Or (to put the point a shade more cautiously) collectively we have found it convenient to impute to our world the degree and the patterns of order that we seem to see in it.

Notice that in imagining how the first humans saw themselves and their world, we have made the mistake of projecting back our own highly elaborated language and world view into *their* situation. I did that in order to explain my theory of how they were first able to develop the earliest beginnings of a common language, a common world, and some measure of subjective consciousness. But it wasn't quite like that *for them*, in those days. *We* weren't hovering around, observing them and understanding them and so helping them to understand themselves. They had only their own immanent point of view, such as it was. They knew nothing of the past, nor of any independent world apart from themselves. All they could be aware of was the first appearance of a small, flickering flame of consciousness in the writhing darkness of animal experience. That for them was the moment of creation: a little light appears in the general darkness. And what does this illumination consist of? It is the very beginnings of a common language and a common world, when in the cry of a fellow member of one's own species one *recognizes* a shared meaning, a wider significance, something in common.

So consciousness depends on language, which in turn depends upon the recognition of something public, something in common, which in turn again depends upon the establishment of shared meanings. To demonstrate the point, lie back and let your mind wander. Consciousness idling consists of running words – and words are public objects. Now try just inventing some new word of your own, and turn it loose: see if it will run along with the other, ordinary words in your vocabulary. It will not. The thing cannot be done. Idling consciousness consists, and consists *only*, of a motion of public objects, ordinary words, somewhere within your system. Consciousness is not something private and 'spiritual' that goes on in the brain: consciousness is simply a secondary effect in us of the motion of the public language. That is why the dawn of consciousness coincided with the first establishment and recognition of common meanings, and it is also why, philosophically speaking, language precedes 'reality'; that is, the public world of linguistic meaning logically precedes *both* the public world of fact *and* the seemingly private world of lit-up subjective consciousness. People usually make a rather sharp distinction between the public and private realms, but language in motion cheerfully disregards it. The public/private distinction *is itself secondary*.

All of this sounds very clear and satisfactory, but philosophy is not easily satisfied. It has long regarded the ordinary life world as a very unsatisfactory world, and has dreamt of escaping from it to find a more real, unchanging, and intelligible world. This dream of an intellectually satisfying noumenal world influenced the way people saw the new mechanistic science that developed in seventeenth-century Europe through the work of Galileo and Newton. The new physics proposed a highly idealized picture of the workings of a physical universe completely describable in terms of matter, motion and number. It was a universe that was, or seemed to be, transparent to reason and fully deterministic. To be sure, complications like air resistance and rolling friction caused bodies in the empirical world not to behave with quite such exact predictability as the model said they would. But it was assumed that the complications could be taken into the calculation, and that the world as described by scientific theory was a clearer, more exact and truer account of the real world out there than the account given in ordinary language. So to this day many scientists can still regard themselves as being like platonic philosophers, leading us towards a truer vision of the real world than the one that is given to us in our ordinary language.

This history explains why for a long time Western thought suspected that although everything in the life world seems to be contingent, the higher truth revealed by science is that every event in the physical world is mechanistically determined. Determinism seemed to be a major problem, and indeed a threat.

Today, we hear much less about determinism. The mechanistic world model thrown up by seventeenth-century science was never more than a highly idealized construct. It was a mistake to suppose that it was a world picture more reliable, more real, and more true than the world picture of ordinary language and everyday life. On the contrary, in order to bring the idealized world of Newtonian mechanics into line with the fuzzier facts of the world of ordinary language and everyday life, we would have to introduce so many qualifications and complications that we would inevitably move over from the clean-cut mechanistic notion of causation to something much more like the Buddhist account. And in any case, the old mechanistic determinism presupposed an exceedingly precise and determinate material world existing 'out there', prior to language, independent of it, and copied by it. But today, language and the world are interwoven, and the world has inevitably come to share language's own fuzziness, indeterminacy and sometimes slippery ambiguity.

So we can forget determinism; and I therefore return to our earlier, language based insistence that everything in life is contingent – which means that it is not meant nor necessitated, but simply happens or befalls. Everything comes to be, and passes away, in time. Everything, including both so-called objective reality and so-called subjective consciousness, is language-mediated and part of a single package. And because everything is outsidelessly part of a single great big shapeless bundle – a package that we ourselves have described and assembled – to my mind the only way to come to terms with **it all** is to say 'Yes' to it all. Try to moralize about **it all** as little as possible, and to complain about one's own fate not at all. Cultivate instead the large, generous spirit of one of those great picaresque artists such as Pieter Breughel or Laurence Sterne. That is the best, the least judgemental or moralistic, attitude to life.

We should **say 'Yes' to life** in all its contingency because it is the accidentalness of life that makes *happy* accidents possible, and that makes innovation and creativity possible. We wouldn't wish the self-replication of DNA always to proceed with precise accuracy, because without all the slippage and the accidents there would not have occurred the favourable mutations on which evolution depends – and so it is also in the realm of language and personal life.

No doubt people's suspicion and fear of universal contingency is related to their fear of death. They imagine – no doubt we all of us sometimes imagine – that on the leading edge of time, where the present is always slipping away into the past, everything is passing away all the time, and we with it. Many people suffer dreadfully from the fear of death, and above all from horror at the thought of being dead oneself. They need a cure; and fortunately there is a cure. In religion, the cure is the practice of solar living. In philosophy, we can urge essentially the same result by offering this advice: Don't think only of the universal passing away of everything. Think also of everything's coming to be. And then give the two thoughts *exactly equal weight*. Contingency is universal passing away *and* universal renewal, going away and coming back, loss and gain, both at once, and as a single package. To accept and affirm universal contingency is to say 'Yes' to the whole package in the recognition that we cannot really imagine things otherwise. How else could it be? Those of us who have learned to love contingency have found that it is precisely the most fragile, ephemeral, and secondary things that move us most deeply, and that we love most dearly.

Chapter 4

Life Exceeds and Laughs at All Our Faiths and Ideologies

Georges Perec (1936-1982) published *Life: A User's Manual*[1] in 1978. It is 'the last major event in the history of the novel', as Italo Calvino called it, an encyclopaedic account of the inhabitants of one Paris tenement house in all the extraordinary variety of their lives and concerns, and one which becomes a microcosm of all human experience. This in turn leads me straight to the objection to be debated now: The human life world is so vast and so endlessly varied and contains so many inconsistencies, extremes and sharp incongruities that it surely cannot be totalized and explained in any one tidy system of general thought. Life contains all the systems – the religions, the philosophies, the works of art, the political ideologies – but it is bigger than any of them. It far exceeds them, and it laughs at them all. What do we make of that?

Might we perhaps respond to this challenge by trying to frame a *Lebensphilosophie*, a philosophy of life, which starts from precisely the features of life that are alleged to make it untheorizable? Maybe – but surely it cannot end up with any more than what Perec has already given us, namely a rather detached, droll and good-humoured description of a typical sample of life's huge, tumultuous variety. No theory of life is going to be able *both* to do full justice to it all *and* to tell us what it all means, and how we should live.

Alternatively, we may admit that life itself is wildly chaotic and excessive in all directions, but then we may go on to say that the job of a particular philosophy or religion – or whatever – is to present us not with the whole truth about life, but only with a contrived image of life, life made sense of in such a way that within this simplified and meaning-rich representation of human life we can each hope to frame a personal faith to live by and create a meaningful performance.

How will a person who takes this line explain and justify her own faith? She'll say: 'If I try to stay true to life itself and as a whole, I'll end up in Perec's position: droll and detached, with a feeling of infinite absurdity. I'll feel overwhelmed: I won't be able actually to *live*. So it seems to me reasonable, for the sake of being ethical and gaining satisfaction from life, to seek out a powerful and wide-ranging art-image of **what life is all about,** and to commit myself to it so that within it I can shape a life and pursue the values that seem most worthwhile to me.[2] It seems to me that life itself is so chaotic and appalling that simply in order to live I've got to cut it down to size and *make* it make a sort of sense'. Thus she admits that we cannot have a conceptually clear philosophical totalization of the meaning of life, but she says we can be content with art-images of life's meaning – conceiving of it, for example, as a great journey, or as a school in which we are preparing for a Final Examination.

By the end of the twentieth century, I suspect, most people in the West had reached the position just described. It implies that we've given up old ideas of divine revelation, and given up the claim that our own religious system is dogmatically just *true* for all human beings everywhere. Instead, the person I have described sees religion as being cultural, and as like art. Most of us humans have at least some residual connexion with an ancestral religious tradition. That tradition gives us, under a group of dominant symbols, a world-view and an account of how we human beings come to be here, how it is with us, and how we should live. Such traditions are in most cases pretty flexible: they can be bent into new shapes and appropriated in new ways. People in other cultures are often so different that it hardly makes sense for me to claim that my tradition is normative for all human beings. But I *can* make the much more modest claim that with a bit of honest effort I can appropriate and bend *my own* tradition in such a way as to make it possible for me to construct a meaningful and value-rich form of life for myself out of it.

That being the case we now see that life is much too vast and various for any one religion or philosophy to be objectively true, everywhere and for everyone. But by working with the stories and symbols that we have inherited, we can still build a house of meaning for ourselves to inhabit. And those in other traditions are fully entitled to do something similar for themselves with the rather different materials available to them.

In the late 1980s I was putting forward a position of this type under the slogan 'active non-realism', and some years earlier one might have cited C.G. Jung and many others as exponents of similar views. But such ideas elicit very serious objections. The first is that although in most traditions the laity are nowadays allowed to get away with practising their religion on this basis, the core religious professionals are everywhere still expected to be – and insist that they are – dogmatic realists, or even fundamentalists. For the sake of certain myths about authority, historical continuity and so on, an appearance of 'authentic', 'literal' belief needs to be strictly maintained amongst the official hierarchy. And without going into too many details, this is a point upon which they are very firmly resolved and indeed quite ruthless. They propose to make sure that non-realism never becomes more than a tolerated weakness.

The second objection to non-realism is that it can produce only a pale simulacrum of the 'great' tradition that preceded it. For evidence, look at the various temples which Asian communities in the West have erected in recent years. They are modern pastiche versions of something that five or ten centuries ago was still great art – but now is merely a cheap mock-up, like a film set. The comedown is devastating. Nobody should wish to continue a once-great religious tradition in such a pallid and tawdry style. Does a non-realist continuation of Christianity manifest a similar spiritual decline? Yes, I fear so. Compare, for example, fifteenth-century Gothic art with its postmodern and non-realistic continuation in the High Victorian Gothic of certain industrial countries. Is there a comparable comedown? Yes. It is not quite as bad as the transplanted Asian travesties, but it's very nearly as bad.

The third objection to a non-realistic but neo-traditional revival of religion as culture is the most serious of all. It is not easy to explain accurately, but its gist is given by the word 'laughs' that was used earlier. Life is endless and outsideless: it so far exceeds all human religions and philosophies that it *laughs* at them – and we more than half sympathize with it. Life makes their pretensions seem absurd.

This point needs to be spelled out. Culture has always sought to differentiate itself from Nature, and human beings have always wanted to claim for themselves a higher cosmic status than that of the other animals. In one way or another religion has almost invariably claimed that humans have affinities, relationships, obligations, and a destiny that 'transcend nature'. Somehow we are called to be bigger than mere life. But since about the time of David Hume, we have begun to feel that there is something absurdly hubristic, and even nonsensical, about such claims. There is no 'other world', nature cannot be wholly transcended, and **nobody is or can be bigger than life**.[3] Life is 'excessive' because *it has no outside*. Nature should be respected, not scorned or beaten down.

Now let us state the point with brutal honesty: Even in the most highly-regarded religious communities today there is still a very strong anti-life impulse. Religious professionals often live under vows that deny normal sociability and commit them to solitude and silence; that deny normal sexuality and commit them to celibacy and chastity; that deny the normal animal and human love of freedom and commit them to absolute obedience, and so on. When it is learnt that in North America or in sub-Saharan Africa a large proportion of Roman Catholic priests regularly break their vows, members of the general public are highly scandalized, as if they had always taken it for granted that such vows are entirely reasonable and practicable, and in the past were normally respected. Historians can point out that in the cases of Buddhism and Eastern Orthodox Christianity, as well as in the case of Latin Christianity, in every period of which we have reasonably complete historical records, chastity vows have been widely broken. In fact, about as much as today. But more fundamentally, many people nowadays smile when they hear that vows of chastity are not being kept. They regard the mutual attraction of men and women as being older, stronger, more sane and more 'real' than the preposterous religious inhibitions and regulations that try to suppress it, but too often merely distort it. They are pleased that 'Nature' or 'Life' always turns out to be bigger than our wretched human attempts to overcome it and transcend it. We cannot master life, we cannot jump clear of it, and we cannot satisfactorily theorize it. As the cliché has it, **life is for living**: only an ethical response is adequate.

When I say, then, that in the last generation or two we have (on the evidence of the idioms that have come into ordinary language) been moving over to a religion of life, I mean not only that we are taking life more seriously, acknowledging its outsidelessness, its endless variety, and its proper claims; I mean also that we increasingly reject the sort of religious ideology that affects to disparage 'the world', 'nature', and 'life' — and indeed purports to transcend them. We seek a religion *of* life, that gives life its due and does not pretend that there is anything outside life.

Images of Life

I have suggested already that life is in a sense 'everything': it is endless and endlessly varied, including – as the wedding vows remind us – riches and poverty, better and worse, sickness and health, and much, much more. Life is so varied and shapeless that the ethical implications of saying 'Yes' to life are not at first obvious. Therefore, in order to make the concept of life more manageable and the precise ethical implications of affirming life clearer, I have suggested that we need reduced working images of life. And in fact they do exist. The situation can be summarized in one sentence:

As the typical images of God portray him as universal King, Lord, Judge, Father and perhaps Lover; so the classic images of Life portray it as Journey, School, Market, Theatre and Elixir (i.e., wine, *élan vital* or *libido*).

The details and the differences here call for comment. In traditional belief the God of monotheism is or was an infinite, transcendent spirit-being. He (clearly a non-sexual 'he' is involved here) is absolutely One. He is the only ground of being, and there cannot be another. He is omnipresent, eternal, immutable and utterly simple. He is omnipotent, perfect and therefore (as one might say) completely actualized. It follows from this brief sketch of his traditional metaphysical attributes that God is everywhere and at all times equally overwhelming and exactly the same, without any change or difference at all. So how can 'belief in the existence of' such a being ever make any difference at all to poor animals like us? How can a finite temporal being like me have any *dealings* at all with Something that can never in any way yield, or gain, or lose, or differ? Surely a god who can never respond, nor even *modulate* his ceaseless activity, may as well not be there at all.

The obvious reply to this is to cite God's traditional moral attributes. God is without any limitation wise, just, and loving. He preplans and watches over all things. But here arises the awkward contrast that whereas life is full of reverses, ups, and downs, God is utterly equable and never budges an inch. And in fact we find that ordinary people never think much about either God's metaphysical attributes or his moral attributes. Instead, they are content to operate with pictures of God that portray him as a very great and idealized version of a human being – a king, lord, judge or father. Here the ethical implications of the images are obvious: we should live *as if* watched over by a perfectly wise and just paternal Providence. And this is not all; for vivid religious experience often runs so close to sexual experience that God is also very commonly pictured in the very different role of a lover. When devotion becomes very warm, the thought of God seems to become very internal and emotionally 'melting', so that religious experience feels subjectively very like female orgasm. In that case people become ready to talk about 'union' with God, and in various ways to blur the normally sharp duality between the self and God, as this more 'liquid' sexual imagery modifies the impression given by the very 'dry' imagery of patriarchal supervision.

So much for the traditional images of God. What of the parallel images of life? Life is surely not in any way a distinct Being over against us. It is not ontologically transcendent, nor is it infinite. Life is temporal and processual. It involves the pursuit of goals, the practice of relationships with others, and a ceaseless buzz of symbolic exchange. This means that whereas the popular images of God invoke a dominant but benevolent controlling and lawgiving personal being, the images of life prefer to use the workings of a social institution within life as an image of life as a whole. And while belief in divine Judgement and life after death remained strong, the most popular images continued to say, 'You should live your whole life as a journey or pilgrimage towards a final consummation that you will reach through death', and 'You should see your whole life as a period of schooling or probation, or even athletic training, in preparation for a great trial or test that awaits you after death'.

These two images, the Journey and the School, were the traditionally approved images of human life in which the individual was
described as *Homo viator*, man the wayfarer. In this life we were said to
be *in via*, on the way: we pass this way just once — heading for somewhere else. Our life, *this* life, was not seen as final and to be loved and
enjoyed just for its own sake, but as merely instrumental and transient.
The other images of life are very much more social and worldly. The
first one says: 'All our life we are living in relations of *exchange* with other
people and with the environment. Don't be too puritanical about the
market. Don't worry about conserving your personal purity and identity. Plunge in, mix it up, enjoy the haggling and the give and take. The
idea that 'the market' is Vanity Fair is quite wrong. Look at your Bronze
Age and Iron Age history: the market place stood next to the Temple, or
was even *in* it. It was *the gods themselves* who gave us money (from the
goddess Juno Moneta) and the rules of commutative justice, or fair trade.

When I quote and extol the image of our social life as a marketplace
in which people are all the time buying and selling, trading and making
deals, I am deliberately reversing centuries of the wretched
puritanism/socialism which regarded money as 'dirty' and the whole
business of buying and selling as too 'low' for a fastidious Christian who
is concerned about moral cleanliness. We have to be similarly aggressive
in reversing the long centuries of moral disparagement of the theatre
and playacting. Life *is* theatre in the sense that it calls upon us every day
to enjoy acting out our various social roles as worker, parent, spouse,
flighty teenager, uniformed public servant and so on. There are dozens,
even hundreds of such roles, and everybody plays many of them every
day. But our historic moral prejudice against acting is revealed in what
we did with the ancient Greek word for an actor: it became 'hypocrite'.
If your moral fear of role-play is as great as that, then you are bound to
conclude that in order to be truly and purely yourself you must withdraw from everyday human life altogether, like a nun or a hermit. But
what *can* be the point of a religious outlook which makes you unable to
function normally in the human life world, the only world we have or
will ever have?

Now, just as in the case of the images of God, the four dominant
patriarchal images of King, Lord, Judge and Father were complemented
and considerably modified by the image of God as a lover who melts
the soul internally, so in the case of life the four images drawn from the
working of various social institutions are complemented and considerably modified by the more mystical and sexual image of life as a heal-
ing, reviving and indeed ecstasy-inducing fluid that enters our bodies

and courses through us. Here we have an interesting mixture of drinks and body fluids. They include *elixirs*, magical potions that induce love or prolong life, *ichor*, the Greek gods' version of blood, *blood* itself, which 'is life', *water, wine* and, associated especially with sparkling wine, *spume*, *froth* and *sea-foam*, which in turn are associated with *spittle*, which was formerly used to heal, and the sacred life-giving fluid, *semen*. Because life is usually, or very often, pictured as a liquid that pulses or spurts within us, a number of these liquids are also associated with spurting. The rhythmic falling of waves on the shore generates foam, and so is associated with the shaking of the champagne bottle, the pulsing of the heart, and the pelvic thrusting of sex.

The imagery here has always been popular, from the birth of Aphrodite from the sea-foam on the beach near Limassol to the drinking song in *La Traviata* (*Viva il vino spumeggiante*), and the celebrations of victorious motor-racing drivers today. It may be thought to be rather 'pagan', but in fact is surprisingly prominent both in the Bible and in standard religious language. Thus the Jews have a toast, on drinking wine: '*L'chayim*' – To life! In the Hebrew Torah God's word 'is your life'[1] – or rather, God *himself* 'is your life, and the length of your days'.[2] In Christian language Christ is 'our life', and the Holy Spirit is the Quickener, the one who makes alive, in the Nicene Creed (*Zöopoietes*). And all this imagery was originally taken much more literally than it is by believers today. Thus in Genesis the Patriarchs still follow the old custom of demanding the swearing of an oath upon the male genitals ('put your hand under my thigh', says Abraham[3]), the point being that the liquid produced there was thought to be charged up with divine life-giving power – and not just metaphorically, but quite literally so.

In ordinary language this notion of life as a highly pleasurable elixir or flow of feeling that gives relish to the daily business of living is invoked in many stock idioms: **it makes me feel more alive, zest for life, Lebensgefühl, enjoy life,** and so forth. The whole world of life is often spoken of as pulsating, with its own rhythm and pace that one needs to keep up with. When we are young, we often find the life drive or sex drive as a source of unhappiness, but when we are old, we know that our living would be unbearably grey and dull without it. In the past people often battled against their own libido to live celibate lives; today we have changed our view so much that if we find that our libido is weak, we go to the doctor for some treatment that will restore it.

Chapter 6

Life Is Sacred

A number of correspondents have written to me[1] to say that the modern turn to life and the tendency to speak of life – just natural life – as being **sacred** and of infinite value is so much a part of ordinary language that it has greatly affected not only religious liberals, but even the most conservative Roman Catholics and Protestants. Thus, Roman polemics about abortion and birth control frequently speak of all **life as sacred** and as **belonging to God,** and the Billy Graham organization during the late 1980s rather surprisingly received an award for its use of the word 'life' (in its advertizing, as I recall). This shows that we should beware of the strain of Nietzschean rhetoric that attacks orthodox Christians in general as 'preachers of slow death' and haters of life. If that charge was ever accurate, it is no longer so. The modern turn to life has by now affected even the most traditionally minded people.

Nevertheless, two questions still remain. First, there is the case of a thoroughgoing religious liberal or modern secular person who holds no supernatural beliefs. Such a person no longer recognizes any fenced-off, distinct, sacred sphere of existence. Her whole world has become secular. Yet she finds, a little to her surprise, that a feeling of 'Presence' or of the Sacred can still crop up, often unexpectedly and in a great variety of situations. In such a case, what *is* the Sacred? Why do we still want to use the word: can our choice of it be rationalized or justified?

The other question concerns the aforementioned conservative believers who – rather surprisingly – seem also to have been infected by our late modern sacralization of life, even though they simultaneously profess still to be drawing the same old line between things sacred and things profane. What is happening to them? Is their use of modern life-talk merely opportunistic, and not seriously meant; or could it be that they themselves are undergoing major religious change of which they are not fully aware?

This last is certainly possible. In my own case, it was only after some months of collecting life idioms and tracing the history of the idea of life that I became fully awake to them. Then I looked back over some of my own writing of a decade or so earlier, and was startled by the sight of many very fruity life idioms – personifying life, speaking of its activity and so forth – of whose import I had had no inkling at the time when I had used them. In the same way it could be that, without their knowing it, the belief systems of conservative believers are about to be blown apart by new forces already detectable in their own language, but of which they are as yet quite unaware.

More of that in a moment. I turn now to the case of thoroughgoing religious liberals like me, who consider that in the modern period the traditional sacred realm has entirely disappeared. It has been swallowed up by the process of secularization. People are no longer able to give a rational assent to the old supernatural doctrines (certainly not, if these doctrines *have* to be understood in a realistic sense). The people I am talking about no longer have any feelings of numinous dread when in holy places, and they no longer tremble at the thought of imminent divine judgement. In their view, what was left of the former sacred world has already been largely handed over to the heritage industry, to be exploited as a tourist attraction – which finally finishes it off, for nothing is so secularizing as tourism. And yet, though all this is true, people like me, at least, still have 'religious experiences' and are still frequently prompted to feel that this or that is sacred. How does this happen?

It happens because of the chronic ambiguity and instability of the great binary contrasts around which so much of thinking has revolved. To take the simplest example, absence can very often come to be experienced as an indirect mode of presence. For centuries we had a strong sense of the universal presence of God in the world: then God died, and we found ourselves in a bleak, empty world from which God had become absent – and then we began to find that the constant aching sense of God's absence feels oddly like a sense of God's presence (just as one can have a strong, awed sense of presence as one steps into an empty house). So the absence of God can turn into, or come to be experienced as, an indirect mode of the presence of God. The process of secularization may at first have seemed utterly to banish God, but it turns out in fact that as the victory of secularization becomes complete, the sacred tends to return – perhaps in indirect and negative form – as one is constantly reminded of its *absence*. Another particularly clear example is the return of the sacred in abstract art. For when in Mark Rothko (and perhaps also in Barnett Newman) the painting as an object becomes completely aniconic, then it turns into a very powerful *icon* of the sacred! Voidness becomes a sign of transcendence.

Something similar happens with the arrangements of rocks and marks on landscape made by the artist Richard Long. Long's creations are quite unlike the traditional obelisks and menhirs, because they are always resolutely horizontal. They *never* point up to the heavens. But this very self-effacing ephemeral quality in Long's work *in itself* has a way of becoming religious.

The biggest shakeup of traditional ideas about the sacred is the one that has accompanied the incremental shifting of religious attention to this world, a process that has been going on in the West since the high Middle Ages, and the gradual turning of philosophical attention towards history and everyday life that has been going on especially since Hegel and Schelling. The classical, predominately celibate Christianity of the first millennium, in alliance with platonism, had always sought to turn people's attention upwards, from things temporal and material towards things invisible, eternal and spiritual. One was urged to turn away from everything that is merely contingent, finite, sensuous, volatile and (in a word) *female*; but the traditional 'platonic' valuations have been gradually reversed over recent centuries, to such an extent that it is usual today for people to be religiously moved by everything that is at the bottom of all the old platonic value-scales – childbirth, flowers, insects, moody feelings, moody weather, shadows and the most transient earthly beauties.

As we break away from platonism and from traditional religious values, religion returns in some very unexpected places. For example, the wilderness was traditionally seen as infested with potentially hostile spirits. One went into the wilderness to be tempted by the devil. But today the wilderness is much more likely to be perceived as holy, virginal and unsullied. More than that, when I have been alone in a vast, inhuman and unnamed arctic wilderness I have been awed by its very god*less*ness.

It is death, it is the void, it has a certain utterly inhuman serenity. In such a place, it is a good religious discipline to stop, and wait in that absolute, unrelieved emptiness. This is pure 'it', the uncanny, the other.[2] It may perhaps be seen as a negative sacred because it is numinous, not in its fulness, but *in its very emptiness*.

I am trying to say that for me and for many others like me, the sacred that returns is not the same as the old sacred that we finally lost some three decades ago, or thereabouts. The sacred that has returned is something like a vast empty otherness that I am made aware of when I am confronted by my own life's utter transience and contingency. Life is so fragile and so precious; it is all we've got, and yet it is nothing and it is a nothing surrounded by nothingness.

Remember that, like death, the negative sacred is not some thing. It is no thing. I know of it only by the way it fills me with dread, that's all. I may, for example, think of the self as a mere series of states, like a string of beads but with no metaphysical string holding the beads together. Or I may think of the world of experience as consisting simply in what we perceive, with no underlying metaphysical order holding it all together. I may say to myself: 'The void starts on the far side of the screen of experience. Beyond my projected sensory impressions and the language that joins them up to compose a world, there is nothing at all – not even Nothingness'. Thoughts like these **put the fear of God into me**; that is, they fill me with a negative dread that is both like and unlike the old sense of the sacred.

The negative sacred, I am saying, is like death and perhaps even *is* death in that (if we are honest) it still fills us with dread even though nowadays we know that there is nothing else. Death is going to sleep and not waking up; death is simply sudden extinction; death is nothing to be afraid of, and we will never know that we're dead. There can be no reason at all for being afraid of death, nor indeed for ever giving it a thought. There is nothing there to think about or prepare for. But, however long one spends reasoning with oneself and trying to get completely free from any dread or anxiety about death, a phrase like 'There is nothing to be afraid of ' still has an odd way of coming to life, rearing up, and looking menacing. So the negative sacred keeps tending to creep back: I have elsewhere associated it with the term 'the it', *der Es*, seeing it as a background sense of something impersonal, elusive, unmasterable and threatening that hovers around the edges of the lit-up life world of intersubjective conversation.

And if indeed death is the negative sacred, then it is obvious that we must come to see life as its positive counterpart. Life is itself the sacred, the awe and dread we feel in contemplating it being compounded of our awareness of its utter contingency – even, its *nihility* – together with our own utter dependence on it, and its continual, determined, busy upwelling and self-affirmation. Watch insects.

So death is the negative sacred and life is the positive sacred, and these two are one. The sacred is not a something; it is our response of awe and dread to everything's utter contingency, and our life's groundlessness or gratuitousness.[3] When people speak of **the first stirrings of life** and of **the miracle of life**, they are speaking of a unique mixture that we are aware of in life's regular self-healing, self-refreshing and self-renewal. It is utterly contingent and spontaneous – and yet it is also reliable, and even regular. Think how hard the Northern winter is for hundreds of species; but every spring they all come back again without fail.

Chapter 7

City Life

Cities have come into being for the first time, in different places and independently of each other, on at least six or eight occasions. The jargon phrase for this is 'primary urban generation', which is said to have occurred in, for example, China, the Indus Valley, Mesopotamia, Egypt, Central and West Africa, and Meso-America at various times during the last 7000 years. Cities are evidently such a good thing that they have been invented several times over, like eyes and wings during the course of animal evolution. And everywhere, I think, the city arises as a focus of regulating *authority*, both religious and political. At the centre of the city is a sanctuary where the god sits enthroned, with perhaps alongside it a royal audience hall or basilica where the king sits enthroned. The king is usually said to be the god's Son, or his earthly representative. People go up to the city to attend an annual cycle of feasts, a cycle which marks out the shape and the main tasks of the agricultural year.

Thus the city becomes a centre from which life in the surrounding agricultural hinterland is regulated. It prescribes the calendar, and issues currency. It may be fortified. It may collect some form of tithes, or levy taxes and men for military service. Its population includes specialist craft-workers – masons, metalworkers, potters and weavers producing goods of interest to visiting farmers. So the city becomes a place of meeting and of business, a place where all sorts of things circulate like blood — gossip, money, news, goods, feelings, tastes, fashions, jokes, opinions, ideas.

The city comes to be thought of as a place where **the pace of life** is rapid, and where life itself is found at its most intense and highly concentrated. Coming to market, the farmer trades his whole year's production, picks up all the gossip, and comes close to the great centre of sacred power.

Whatever 'life' is, then, it is at its most highly concentrated and moves at the fastest pace in the city. When we are comparing life with blood, we may speak of it as a process of *circulation*; when we compare it with money, we may speak of *currency* (literally, running around); and when we have the motion of a living language in mind, we may describe life as a continual process of exchange, and especially *symbolic exchange*, trading words. Although it might well be thought that every living human being is equally **in the midst of life**, in fact we feel a strong need to **keep in touch** by visiting the city regularly, and listening out for news of what's going on there. For if we neglect to maintain our very delicate social attunement with other members of our group, we soon begin to fear that **life will pass us by**. We will be 'behind', **out of touch, out of the loop**. Perhaps the whole business of women's fashions in dress is the clearest example of how the whole of culture works — including the state of the language, our common construction of the world, public opinion, public taste, morality, knowledge, and the rest. Everything works very much as the business of women's fashions works. And if that example be thought insufficiently exalted, then we may say that everything works as the stock market works. Everything, be it linguistic meanings or truths or valuations, is created and sustained within a highly flexible human consensus that is endlessly *traded* and renewed — and shifts a little every day.

Furthermore, when we visit the city we are not just absorbing the latest news and the latest fashions, and generally getting ourselves up to date: we are also doing a little bit of business on our own account. A little trading, or a little display. One wants to be seen, so one parades oneself; or one wants to do a little dealing — the point being that one **brushes up** one's knowledge of the current symbolic language in order to be able to *compete* effectively. We need to keep our own feelings in tune with the fashion. We want to attract a little more attention than others are getting; we trade in order to gain business advantage. Thus we are social beings in a dual sense: we love to *conform* and we love to *com-*

pete. We want to be just the same as all the others, and to know just what they all know, so as to give ourselves the best chance of doing a little bit *better* than all the others. The better we learn the current language, the more effectively we can make our own statement in it. We work to become and to remain very delicately attuned to the current idiom – in order that by using it more skilfully than our neighbours, we can gain some small advantage over them. So society is a forum, a grand parade, a marketplace and a theatre. **That's life**, and we wouldn't for a moment have any of it otherwise, or different in any way. No doubt a biologist would say that it is all grounded in sexual selection – the competition amongst animals for the best mating opportunities.

Now a paradox: we began by remarking that the city originated as a centre of sacred authority. This is the place where the god first set the world in order. This is the place where he has chosen to set his great name. This is the place where he still sits enthroned in his great house. Here too the king who is his son and servant also sits enthroned, ruling in his name. From this centre sacred power radiates out over the surrounding country, the kingdom being the territory over which the king's writ runs.

So the city is basically the seat of the god's power, perhaps largely or partly delegated to the king who rules in his name. But our brief discussion led us instead to a very different story of the city, as a hectically-busy place of *human* assembly, display, trade and debate. In the Temple the priests will tell you that one thing and one thing only has called human society into being and keeps it together, and that is the legislative power and authority of the Creator God. But out in the forum or marketplace next to the temple you may well feel prompted to tell an entirely different story about how human society works and sticks together, a story that tells of how intensely sociable we are and how much we love life – life being a matter of gossip, of parading in one's new hat, of haggling in the marketplace, and of keeping oneself up to date and **in the know**.

The priests in the temple dislike the noisy goings-on outside in the agora. They have successfully imprinted upon our whole tradition a strain of vehement religious disapproval of money, of business and the market, of gossip and fashion, and of the theatre. Religion and absolute monarchy have always claimed to represent to us an authoritative unchanging superhuman order – the law, morality, sacred things. They have always feared and have intensely disliked everything that I am calling *life* – everything that is only human, highly mutable, emotive, and transactional. They insist upon the timeless greatness and beauty of the god, and declare that we are utterly dependent upon him. But I am suggesting that ever since cities began, there has been another story that says the whole of culture is purely immanent and ungrounded. It depends upon – and *only* upon – our intense sociability and our astonishing capacity for mutual attunement. For an example of this consult some entries in a dictionary that stresses current usage, and see in what fine detail you already know – and we all of us know – *exactly* how words are currently being used. Or consider how quickly even relatively poor and disadvantaged young people are able to pick up and adopt the latest fashions, and can somehow intuit what sort of delightful absurdities you can and cannot get away with just now. Consider, again, how the common language changes continuously, how it is often wiser than individuals are, and how much of our thinking it does for us.

It looks as if two rival philosophies have coexisted and have battled against each other since cities began. One thinks in terms of unconditional authority, tradition and cosmic monarchy. All the standards that we need to live by emanate from a superior legislating authority whose seat is in the sacred world. But the other philosophy is life-centred and radically democratic. Everything, but *everything*, is contingent: everything arises within a living human consensus that is always undergoing renegotiation – in the media, in the marketplace, and in every other arena where human beings interact.

Some people will object sharply to this account. They dislike the implications of the ideas of radical contingency and thoroughgoing immanence, and doubt if it even makes sense to say that we ourselves have evolved amongst ourselves and are the only makers of world-view, religion, morality, art, and indeed rationality itself. They point out that nearly always Academies and similar professional bodies control subject-areas, and that the sovereign person or body in the State nearly always finds it necessary to regulate the market – at least, to some extent. To this we reply that questions of market regulation are *themselves* also the subject of continual public debate in free societies nowadays, so that we have in fact already made any transcendent regulator redundant. We ourselves constantly think up and try out new systems of regulation.

The critics have another point to make: they have always regarded the endless motion and self-criticism of the 'transactionalist' or 'market' vision of the world as 'futile' and 'meaningless'. In a radical democracy, society just goes on talking to itself, criticizing itself, and 'reforming' itself piecemeal, for ever. No ultimate end, no absolute truth, no final resting-place is ever reached; and this seems to the critics to suggest that human beings are like the damned in Dante's *Inferno*: driven by their own vain desires, they just run round in futile circles. Our life is a great turning wheel that never gets anywhere. The pendulum swings back and forth, and the fashion changes – but there is no *progress*, because we have no extrahuman fixed standard against which to measure our own progress or regress.

According to these critics the residual monarchy, the residual monotheism, the residual dogmatic rationalism, and in short the residual platonic 'realism' of modern Western societies is no accident. It is our last remaining defence against thoroughgoing immanence, galloping relativism, and moral collapse. We must *cling* to what's left of the old god and the old certainties.

So it is said: and it is precisely at this point that various sorts of fundamentalism and right wing authoritarianism slip in the knife, and begin to work their way back into public acceptance and even on to the high moral ground of contemporary public debate. How can this happen? It can happen because religious and moral disapproval of the marketplace, the theatre, the fashion parade, and, quite simply, *traffic* and busy-ness has been so intense for so long. That it is still alive even today reminds us how original and how wonderful is the frank pleasure in the visual buzz and dynamism of street life that we see in Camille Pissarro's city paintings.[1] These paintings include one (*Place Saint-Lazare*, 1893) which has been described as 'the first serious study of traffic in the history of art',[2] a phrase which might better be used of the artist's whole body of work during the decade of the 1890s.

Pissarro in his old age looks at the life of Paris with straightforward pleasure in its teeming, varied business and busy-ness. He was one of the first to be quite free from the old assumption that the City of Man is hellbent and that city life is all vanity and futility.[3] After him, the old disapproval could still return – for example, in the rather suspicious reaction of the critics to Piet Mondrian's 'Boogie Woogie' paintings, done in New York in the early 1940s. How could the old puritan have permitted elements of pleasure in the vitality of New York life to enter his famously austere art? In Jacques Tati's last film, *Traffic* (1972), one is aware of mixed feelings about the crowded cars turning about a *rond-point*. Is this a carousel, or are we watching the futile circular motion of damned souls in Dante's *Inferno*? The latter image seems to prevail. Apparently we still don't like ourselves very much: we are apt to eye with some disgust any large assembly of people, travelling, partying, at the market, on the beach. But **that's life**. Perhaps we should forget the point of view of those older people who are becoming **tired of life**, and should remember instead the eager young person who declares that she's bored with her rather slow village surroundings. She wants to **see life**, which means 'see the world', which means 'go to town'.

Chapter 8

A Dog's Life

Human thinking is almost always at first heterological, remarks Slavoj Zizek. We somehow recoil from thinking about any big topic in a head-on and straightforward way. So instead of thinking directly about what (for example) consciousness is, we had to start by thinking about God or about some alternative great other, and then we thought about how very uncomfortable and self-conscious we are made by that great eye – or I – looking at us. The first forms of self-consciousness were the awareness of oneself as a sinner before God, and the awareness of oneself as having been *found out*, caught in some indiscretion or other embarrassing bit of misbehaviour. The consciousness of sin, or of acute embarrassment, is much easier to recognize and think about than pure self-consciousness or reflection. What on earth *is* a spirit's ability to see itself without any physical mirror? I don't know; but I do know very well what it feels like to have been found out. I'm a married man: I can never get away with anything.

The nature of self-consciousness is a daunting question to tackle head-on. So we had to dramatize it and think it *indirectly*, *via* another. That makes it manageable – and, by the way, we just stumbled upon the chief reason why for thousands of years belief in God has seemed so easy and natural to millions of people. The idea of God and the god's-eye view of things may seem frightening in some ways, but it has the considerable merit of giving us an agreeable and comfortable way of thinking about many of the great questions of life. When it comes to ethics, for example, normal people hate to get embroiled in moral philosophy. They somehow can't think straightfowardly about how we should live. So instead of 'What shall I do?', they ask the seemingly clearer and easier question: 'What does God want me to do?', or 'What am I supposed to do?'

Now ask the great question: What *are* we? What is a human being? Answer: we are stumped. We have no idea even of where to look for the right vocabulary in which to frame an answer. Against what should we be measuring ourselves, in what context do we belong? It is not obvious. In order to make progress, we are forced to try rephrasing the question in heterological terms: How do we human beings differ from other animals? *Now* the question suddenly becomes answerable. From the earliest times we can trace, our relation to mammals in particular has been of very great importance to us. We have hunted them, we have depicted them – and ourselves with them – in art, and we also have noted the minutely detailed homologies in anatomy and in behaviour between them and us. The parts of the body, sexual reproduction, the rearing of offspring, social interactions – in all these things we and they are so intimately alike that we clearly *are* animals. Our lives are animal lives, our life cycle is a mammal's life cycle. So throughout history the easiest way for the mass of human beings to think about the question of what a human being is has been for us to ask ourselves how it is that we are animals – who yet differ radically from all the other animals.

There is more: religion in all ages has been really *intensely* preoccupied with the difference between humans and other animals.[1] Religion has always actively *commanded* us to purify ourselves and to grow in holiness by differentiating ourselves – and, what is more, clearly *distancing* ourselves – from other animals. We are animals whose task in life is to become something much *more* than animals. We impose upon ourselves very elaborate codes of religious law, for example, in connection with food and sex, which we wouldn't dream of imposing upon animals. We battle for our human self-realization and self-mastery by controlling, or even repressing altogether, almost everything animal in ourselves, as if we really believe that in order to perfect our humanity we have got to conquer our animality.

This denial of our own animality – and especially, the obvious mammalian character of the human female reproductive apparatus –

has been taken to absurd and grotesque lengths not only in our religious tradition, but also and more recently in our secular tradition. We are all well-accustomed to deploring the Christian and other ascetical traditions that in the past too often alienated religious women from their own sex, their own bodies and their own emotions; but the secular tradition in many ways still continues the same themes – especially when the pursuit of the recently invented cultural fetish 'sex' is taken so far as to amount to a denial of our biology, as when caesarean section becomes more common than natural childbirth, and breasts are given strange unnatural shapes by cosmetic surgery in a society where it nevertheless remains difficult for a woman to breast-feed her own baby in a public place.

Apparently, we are still trying to realize and fulfill our humanity by denying and repressing our animality, and women are still bearing the main burden by having to do their best to live up to impossibly dainty and fluffy ideals of 'femininity'. Animals also suffer, as one sees not only in the continuing pejorative use of terms like 'animal', 'beastly', 'brutish' and so on, but also in our very strong traditions of simultaneously loving and despising dogs and pigs.

It is against this background that we can detect a certain continuing ambivalence in our use of the word life. Right up to Kierkegaard (and perhaps beyond) the Western tradition has preferred to speak of existence rather than life, and to speak of human existence not in biological terms, but in masculine terms of reason and the will, decision and moral action. Before the twentieth century there was little discussion of the complex currents of biological feeling on which our selfhood rides, or of our rich and varied life of kinaesthetic bodily sensations. (The word *kinaesthesia* is of late nineteenth-century origin; we have scarcely noticed, even yet, that we possess *far* more than the traditional five senses.) We still do not much discuss the way our view of everything is shaped by where we stand in the biological life-cycle, and in the wars between the sexes, the generations, and so on. We are still neither fully awake to nor reconciled to our own biology for the excellent reason that it reminds us of too much else that we prefer not to think about: the messiness of life, our corruptibility, our transience, our mortality. The modern turn to life, to the emotions and the senses and the body, especially since Darwin and in writers such as D.H. Lawrence and Freud, shows us struggling to become reconciled to life, to the body, and to this world. But we have to overcome many old obstacles and inhibitions, and the process is still not complete. Samuel Beckett, perhaps the most important twentieth-century writer, remained severely pessimistic about life to the end of his days. With such a predecessor, any major artist who wants to come out on the side of life has a duty to avoid prettifying or idealizing life. One must tell the truth; one must *earn* the right to affirm life. And in their way figures as diverse as Lucien Freud and Ted Hughes did just that. In the future, at the very least, we shall need to work our way towards moral consistency in our treatment of animals, towards a proper understanding and acceptance of our own animal background and constitution, and towards a view of life that has looked life's transience, messiness, arbitrariness and cruelty in the face – and yet still says a full religious Amen to it.

It's My Life

Sometimes we speak of life in general as being like a great river that we all swim down together. Life in this sense is common, public. We each enter and leave it at different points, but while we are in it we are all in it together.

At other times, however, we speak of life in a very privatized way: **my life**, in the sense of my personal lifespan. To a young person who has a long, open future in prospect and who must take career decisions, we may say, **You've got your whole life before you**. Another person may claim the right to decide for herself **what I want to do with my own life**. She speaks of herself as the rightful owner of her own life: **It's my life**, she says, **I have the right to control my own life**. She feels so strongly about it that she may be ready to run away from home or even commit suicide, rather than submit to an arranged marriage. In short, we are talking here about something like a new religion, for which many young people are willing to face *martyrdom*.

The dual central motifs of this new religion seem to be the vital need to maintain one's own self-respect – '**I wouldn't be able to live with myself** if I were to do that' – together with the imperative need to assume full moral responsibility for one's own life. Conservative anti-humanists are apt to make scornful remarks about the 'me' generation and about the wilfulness and self-absorption of the young, but in fact the notion that our first concern should be for our own personal salvation is characteristic not only of early Christianity (e.g., *Philippians* 2:12) but also of several other strands in 'Axial Age' religion – Buddhism, for example.

Nevertheless, we should note that an ancient idea has here been given a new and characteristically modern twist; for only in modern times have people come to think of themselves as the owners of their lives with the right to shape those lives as they think fit – by adopting an individual **lifestyle** of their own choice, by **sharing their lives** with **life-partners** of their own free choice, and so on. How you want to shape your own life is evidently of great religious significance, because the old *spiritual director* of the past, whose scope was limited to the sphere of your religious life, has now been replaced by the **life coach** whose scope is more or less unlimited. He helps you to sort out your priorities, and take charge of your life. These claims are indeed as momentous as they are novel; I can *contemplate* my life as a whole; I can *claim* myself as its only rightful owner; I have a moral right and duty to *shape* it, to *style* it in the way that suits me; my chief task in life is to *make the best I can* of my life, so that at the end of my life I'll be able to look back with some satisfaction and think that **I gave it my best shot**. My life needs to become something like a work of art in which I have fully expressed myself.[1]

Evidently we have each of us come to think this way; my life is all I've got. I *must* assert my own personal ownership of it, and my right to **do my own thing with my own life**. What is new here is that until quite recently my life, like all other life, did not belong to me: it **belonged to God**. Only God could see my life as a whole. He had determined the date of its beginning, and only he knew when it would end. God alone through his Providence managed or supervised my life. I contributed individual moral acts performed by me, and they were indeed very important. But it was God alone who joined them all together and put them in context as elements within the whole **story of my life**. Only God knew how to make me what he wanted me to be. I couldn't do it all by myself. Thus the whole notion of **my life** remained strongly God-centred until a couple of generations ago. Only in the last century or half-century have most of us come instead to think of *ourselves* as the morally responsible creators and rightful owners of our own lives, and as the planners of our own futures. Today, people even choose their own long-term goals – their fates, their destinies.

How has this new ethic of **my life** become possible? Everyone is familiar with the usual story about the development of Western culture since the Renaissance: the turn to this world, the rise of critical thinking, the explosive growth of new knowledge, natural science and technology, the liberal-democratic state, the re-ordering of all world views, cultures and knowledge around the human subject; the growth of awareness that we ourselves are the builders of all these things; and finally the end of metaphysics and the death of God. That story has been told often enough, but when in addition we take account of the recent **turn to life,** a number of other points come into view as well. Modern medicine, liberal democracy and the emancipation of women have made the average person's life – and especially the average *woman*'s – nearly twice as long and much more predictable. Great social changes have already more than doubled the average life expectancy, and Western women have to a great extent gained control over their own fertility and their own bodies. It has become very much easier than it was in the past to envisage one's lifespan as a whole, to plan it, and to feel morally responsible for it. Every human life remains liable to disruption by accident, illness and political disaster; but since we developed the notion of probability in the seventeenth century, we have become able (at least to some extent) to calculate the likelihood of these misfortunes and to insure against them. In this context, the claim that we nowadays can and must take full control of our own lives no longer sounds like an arrogant fantasy: for most people, most of the time, it seems like common sense. And that people are thinking in these terms is not necessarily a sign that they have become completely irreligious. It may better be read as a sign that nowadays the chief focus of religious attention is upon my relation to my own life.

This is it: I am under a *sacred* obligation fully to appropriate my own life. I must not let it drift, or give away the responsibility for directing it. I am my life, and my life is me, my whole expressed or enacted self. In the past, people often thought of morality as bringing a particular individual life under general rules. Morality didn't at all help you to become your own unique self. Its concern was always to subordinate the particular to the universal. Rule-based morality is therefore dead, because it does not help one to become an individual. Today, we seek to gain *life-satisfaction* by each of us making a unique individual contribution to the human world at large – a formulation which shows why since 1970 morality has to such a great extent been replaced by **lifestyle**. I am under a sacred obligation to find and follow the personal lifestyle through which, as I live it out, I can become a unique, individual, fully-expressed self. It is in that way, and *not* by confining myself to some set of rules, that I can make my best contribution to the human scene as a whole. Perhaps the underlying idea is that the more varied our individual lives, the richer the common world that we will all of us together build.

I need to insist here that I am *not* going back to anything like Kierkegaard's individualism and his very highly 'inwardized' notion of 'subjectivity'. In his earlier 'aesthetic literature' Kierkegaard commends the selfhood of a spy, a man with a dual identity. Such a man's true self is not the one expressed in the outer life he seems to be living, but is a second, hidden, interior self that is supremely conscious and exists only in and for its 'vertical' relation to God. Kierkegaardian individualism requires us largely to reject life: so far as one's outward or social life is concerned, it is enough to go through the motions; the path to true selfhood requires us secretly to cultivate extreme inwardness, intensified subjectivity – in a word, ultra-high *anxiety*.

The Kierkegaardian way to true selfhood first splits us into outer appearance and inner reality, and then follows the path of inwardization. The way to selfhood that I am commending here moves in the opposite direction, by going continually out into social life – which entails symbolic expression. It's a way of continual, and complete, self-outwardization. Whereas Kierkegaard withdrew from life in order to concentrate his attention upon his relation to God, I seek to engage myself completely in my lived, expressed life. As for the alleged interior self, I just don't believe in it. I used to; but not anymore.

In short, I now reject the idea that my chief task is to live a life of conformity to universal moral laws, because I reject the idea that life is valueless in itself, and can gain value only by the way it exemplifies some universal ideal. Instead, I now think that the human task is to live a life that is fully one's own, and not quite like any other. Each of us can and should make a small but unique personal contribution to the fabric of humanity taken as a whole.

Life Must Go On

In the aftermath of the most terrible and tragic events it may at first seem to us that we are going to need a very long period of mourning and readjustment. We can't yet even *think* about returning to normality: it seems that things can never again be the same. We need to gather and bury our dead, we need to care for the survivors, we need time to assimilate what has happened, we need to erect memorials and show all due respect to the dead. And yet, even in these circumstances, people soon begin to acknowledge that above all else we must maintain the continuity of ordinary life. They say, **Life must go on**.

That is extraordinary. We are talking about the most traumatic events, occurrences that above all others *sober* us and demand time and care and observance of ritual proprieties. Yet even such events quickly yield to a still greater and more sacred imperative: **ordinary life must go on**. Whatever happens, or is about to happen, however dreadful, the duty to keep ordinariness going is greater and more sacred still. Amazingly, *ordinariness is the biggest thing there is*. Nothing can displace it. Whatever has happened, **life must go on**, and people know it.

For example, Isaac Bashevis Singer somewhere remarks on the moral grandeur of those Jewish mothers in the early 1940s who battled on, thinking only about where their children's next meal was coming from and peeling potatoes, right up to the end, Holocaust or no Holocaust.

Even when it is obvious to all that life *isn't* going to go on, but on the contrary is going to end unpleasantly some time very soon – *even then* people still behave in every way as if the **must** in the phrase **life must go on** expresses a sacred and unconditional obligation. Ordinariness *must* be maintained. One is conscious of that obligation in the case where one parent continues to feed and bathe the children and put them to bed, while the other parent lies dying in hospital. Life must go on: at times one sees clearly that the duty to maintain the ordinary routines of life is greater and more sacred than the most sacred things of all. 'Life', whatever it is, is bigger even than religion. Now, *explain that thought!*

A second example: after the events of September 11, 2001 in lower Manhattan, political leaders of course had to say that the people of New York and of the whole country must and would respond appropriately. They would gather their dead and mourn them, they would clear up, they would repair and rebuild, and they would in due course prepare an appropriate response. Everything that needed to be done would be done, and done in full. But at the same time – indeed, within a day or two – everyone was also aware that the economic life of the great City must be maintained. The Stock Exchange and similar institutions must be reopened very quickly, and people should think about patronizing the theatres and the thousands of small businesses. It takes a special sort of courage to carry on 'as usual' or 'regardless' at such a time, but one must not be overwhelmed; one must fight back by reaffirming ordinariness. Some events are so daunting and terrible that we have to tell ourselves *both* that we will respond to them by doing all that has to be done with due dignity – *and* that we must not allow these events to weaken our will to live, but will insist upon carrying on 'as if nothing has happened'.

That is odd: we are pledging ourselves *both* to treat with all due seriousness the events that have befallen us *and* – a moment later – to disregard them, putting them out of our minds, and not letting them blow us off course. We will *both* fulfill all our religious duties to the dead and so on, *and* maintain the continuity of ordinary life. If you have worked as a social worker or a city priest you will have done something like this when you have gone from a tragic deathbed to a wedding breakfast within a few hours, and have found that you must join sincerely in the general mood at *both* occasions. **Life's like that** – it is indeed apt to force violent incongruity upon us. Here an interesting theoretical question has just arisen: How can we say that the duty to maintain the continuity of ordinary life expressed in the phrase 'life must go on' is unconditional and overriding, and may even be said to be greater than the duties of religion and of piety towards the dead?

Roughly, we have found that the world of 'life' includes everything: it *includes* all the religions and all the philosophies.[1] There is nothing outside the world of life, and therefore nothing bigger than life. Life exceeds all else, and is not itself exceeded by anything. The obligations that life as such imposes upon us seem to be overriding, and even greater than those of religion.

One explanation of the apparent paradox here is that the primacy of life is a simple matter of our own biological programming. *Of course* living things put survival first; *of course* life is interested from first to last simply in its own self-affirmation, its own burgeoning and multiplication. There wouldn't *be* living things in the world unless life were like that. And, life being like that, so are we.

Fair enough: and, interestingly, religion itself often acknowledges the primacy of life by warning overenthusiastic believers not to court martyrdom, not to be excessively scrupulous, and not to ruin their health permanently by excessive asceticism. Both Catholic Christianity and Middle-Way Buddhism are insistent upon these points.[2] Furthermore, Thomas Aquinas, Spinoza, and other writers are well aware of the sense in which *life*, like health, rationality and sanity, is *transcendental*. In medieval thought, things transcendental are things that are always presupposed. Every true affirmative judgement about the world presupposes that certain ideas about existence, thinghood, truth and so on are already in place. Similarly, every true moral judgement about me and what I have done or ought to be doing presupposes that I, Cupitt, am healthy, sane, rational – and, of course, *alive*. So life is transcendental in the sense that, from the very life-centred human point of view that I've been talking about, the life world is always the starting point and *life is therefore always presupposed*. In which case, *of course* life comes first: for if we are not alive, then as far as we are concerned there is no life world, nobody is doing or saying anything, and nothing matters at all to anyone. There is nobody for anything to matter *to*.

Again, fair enough, but simply to say that life is transcendental, or always already there, is not quite adequate to meet the point we were making earlier about the *sacred* and *over-riding* character of the duty to maintain the continuity of ordinary life. Of course life is always presupposed, and of course life cares only for itself and always *tries* to go on; but what about the solemn *must* in **ordinary life must go on**?

We are talking now about life in the sense of ordinary *human* life, and will argue that not merely is *life* a transcendental – something that is always presupposed – but, more strongly, that everything depends upon and is grounded in ordinary human life and language. For reasons which Wittgenstein was the first to set forth, it is in human ordinariness that language is on its home ground, its birthplace. And thus everything – including all linguistic meaning, accepted truth, and consciousness itself – goes back to and presupposes ordinariness. In ordinariness and in ordinary language is the beginning of the whole world. We all of us began there: there it was that we were first inducted into the human life world and our own linguistic community, and we never leave that starting point wholly behind. We are all rooted in ordinariness.

So it is that the world of ordinary human life and language is the site that in mythology is called the primal mound – the place where dry land first appeared after the primal flood, the place of creation, the site where everything was and is originally set in order.[3] Ordinariness is (logically) the Beginning, and it is always presupposed. That is why it has the special sacredness and authority ascribed to it in the affirmation **Life must go on**. Ordinariness is our indispensable anchorage: without it we are nothing and nowhere.

It is in this realization that the special late modern merging of the sacred and the profane has taken place, and is to be understood.[4] In terms of standard, traditional religious thought, ordinariness is merely the secular, the common, the profane. But the Reformation began, and the twentieth century completed, a dramatic revaluation of ordinariness – expressed typically in talk about the **'sanctity' of marriage**, **of the home**, of **domestic life**, of **life**, of **privacy**, of **human rights** and so on. Ordinariness itself and as such becomes sacred. The rise and spread of such talk marks both the end of the old sacred/profane distinction and the rise of a new religious humanism of this world and of ordinary life.

This perception of the religious weight of ordinariness can deliver people from the tyranny of various sorts of spiritual elitism and petty celebrity worship. A few years ago a London media star who had become very rich and famous at a very early age suddenly began to drink wildly and soon crashed into obscurity. The only explanation proffered for his self-destruction was his remark to a friend: 'I've been to the top and there's nothing there'.[5] It's a good saying, which captures both the ambitious person's belief that at 'the top' he'll find a special personal clarity, fulfillment and security – and his subsequent disillusionment. 'The top', in the sense of a pinnacle of personal achievement, is not a bit like that, and that a certain person for some while stood there can often be recognized only by others, and only in retrospect. And 'the top' as a peak of personal religious happiness and well-being? The person I am talking about sought it in entirely the wrong place. It is accessible to everyone, for the top is to be found in the midst of ordinary life.

Chapter 11

The Pace of Life

Lady Elliot, of Kellynch-hall in Somersetshire, was 'an excellent woman', Jane Austen tells us, whose misfortune it was to have married a desperately boring man. But for seventeen years she had tried her best to make something bearable of him, 'and though not the very happiest being in the world herself, (she) had found enough in her duties, her friends, and her children, to attach her to life'.[1]

What is life, and why does one need to be 'attached' to it? For Jane Austen life is the going-on of things in the social world, and especially in places like Bath where mothers and daughters are always on the look-out for eligible young men. In Jane Austen's day a woman who enjoyed the task of managing a household, raising children, and getting them safely married off usually reckoned that she had enough to live for. Perhaps we should not look down on her, for even today there are plenty of people who would be very glad to have that much.

In the traditional world of women, 'life' seemed to consist largely of observing, interpreting, and discussing events, as well as planning them and attempting discreetly to guide them to a satisfactory conclusion. Because so much was at stake for them, 'life' for women was competitive (highly competitive, some would suggest) but less overtly so than life in the world of men, where images of struggle and conflict are much more prominent. Men who enjoy life are usually men who hugely enjoy what is variously called **the fray** or **the thick of things**. They love being **in touch, in the loop, on the net** and **in public life**, so much that men of affairs – politicians, journalists, traders, fashion and media people, captains of industry and the like – are often very reluctant to retire altogether. They cling on for as long as they can, often long after their accumulated 'wisdom' has ceased to be of any value to the younger generation. They love the buzz, the adrenalin, the sense of being **where it's at**, in the place where the **movers and shakers** make things happen. And it is probably the reluctance of these men **to tear themselves away** from **the place where the action is** that gives rise to talk of **attachment to life** and **clinging to life**.

How do such people think of 'life'? What are they clinging *to*? They speak of life as having its own **pace** or **pulse**, which is alleged to beat more rapidly in the city than in the country. The rapid circulation of ideas and fashions, news and money in the city gives people the impression of the circulation of blood and hormones in the body of a large superorganism, and those who most **love life** want to remain plugged into it. It seems that people who spend their days in the places where life is lived **in the fast lane** – that is, most intensely, and at the most rapid pace – drink in an intoxicating daily charge of energy or vitality. They love it. They are hooked on it. They won't give it up voluntarily. They seem to be vitalists, realists about 'life', for whom life is a sort of fluid like caffeine, adrenaline, or alcohol, of which they demand their daily fix.

How seriously can we, or should we, take such ideas? I suggest that we should follow the biologists in their traditional hostility to vitalism. Just as biological life is not an added quality over and above the chemistry that composes it, so social life is not something independent of the crowd of human beings who generate it. People who fear that they are being outpaced often say that it is hard to keep up, and sometimes claim to fear that **life is leaving them behind**, all of which may give the impression that life is an independent being with its own (uncomfortably rapid) tempo of movement. But that is not how it is. What happens is that we all of us take pleasure in showing how quickly we can **catch on**, by instantly adopting the latest fashions, idioms and ideas, and the speed with which some of the youngest people **catch on** is apt to leave the rest of us gasping in their wake. But we don't like to admit that their youth makes them quicker on the uptake than we are, and so we blame **the pace of life**.

Life is us. It is a function of our intense sociability. We strike sparks off each other, stimulate each other, prompt each other to be creative. And this is especially true in capital cities, where the most talented people congregate – as is shown by the extraordinarily wide gap between metropolitan and provincial art. The excitement of creativity and of being at the centre of things is so great that one can well understand why people become addicted to it, and cling to it.

However, if we are to be non-realists about life, what do we love when we love life, and what do we cling to when we cling to life? It is very important here that we shall not overlook or neglect to cultivate the simple, biological and generally available pleasures of life. They are the pleasure that comes from health and the simple workings of our own physiology; the pleasure we find in all sense experience, in change, and in novelty; and the pleasure that we all have in meeting and conversing with our fellows. The philosopher Richard Wollheim, in a discussion of these elemental pleasures of life, once used the slightly-puzzling word 'phenomenology'. I think he meant to evoke the ever-changing flux of phenomena that life presents to us from moment to moment. He wanted to say that we take great pleasure in the mere flux of our experiences, but I prefer to use the simpler expression, 'the pleasures of life', and want to stress as strongly as I am able how much we need to attend to them and cultivate them. For thousands of years human beings were so savagely disciplined by laws, by religion, and by morality that they very largely lost touch with their own senses, their own bodies, and **the joy of life**. And a great deal of re-discovery yet remains to be done.

Chapter 12

Life Is Not Fair

From time to time we hear people saying sombrely, or in tones of bitter complaint, that **Life's not fair**, that **Life's a lottery**, and that **There's no justice in life**.[1] The making of these remarks implies that some people have had a shock. They expected that life *would* be fair; they expected there to be a moral Providence at work in the world, seeing to it that in the long run villains get what they deserve and good people are vindicated; but their expectations have been rudely disappointed. Why? Why is life not as it should be?

The reply to this is obvious: Why do so many people have such unjustified expectations? Why do people *expect* life to be fair? Do they somehow expect the Universe at large to enforce the principles of morality? Do we really suppose ourselves *entitled* to expect fairness? Clearly, we do not really believe all this, because every developed human society known to us has always had elaborate man-made legal and penal systems, together with many other social arrangements expressly designed to act as moral sanctions by rewarding the good people and punishing the bad. The very fact that we are all of us convinced of the necessity for this manmade machinery to enforce at least a minimum of moral behaviour proves that we do not really suppose that an all-powerful, all-wise, and benevolent Providence is already and independently doing the job for us. If such a God were efficiently enforcing the moral law all the time, there would be no need for any human assistance. But the real position seems to be that the human contribution is much more than merely complementary; it is absolutely vital if we are to sleep safely in our beds at night — so vital that it needs religious support. Religious conservatives, especially those who have a great deal of their own property to worry about, are therefore vehemently insistent that it is the duty of schools and churches to support law and order in human society by teaching backup myths about a cosmic moral order to the young and the poor.

All this suggests that in the past many people did not literally believe in a cosmic moral order already laid on and working, but rather that the function of religion and morality is to defend the rich and old against the envy of the young and poor. In our hearts we always knew perfectly well that civil peace is maintained by the joint operation of various sanctions, ranging from the fear of Hell, through the fear of the gallows, to fear of our neighbours' disapproval — the traditional 'religious', 'civil' and 'popular' sanctions. If these sanctions were not firmly maintained and the moral order broke down, then life would become a chaotic battlefield on which it was every man for himself. That prospect is so horrible that we could all see that we must support the work of our local police department and our local church. Since we didn't really believe in a cosmic moral order, we were convinced that the best deterrent for villains is the fear of God in their hearts, and the certainty that the police will catch them and the courts will punish them.

From this discussion so far I conclude that we never held a straightforwardly realistic belief that there is an all-knowing and completely efficient moral Providence at work in the world. But we have always thought it necessary and expedient to teach myths to that effect to the young and the poor. In particular, we take care to bring our children up in a peaceful, morally governed little sub-world — the world of the nuclear family, the primary school and the local church. So far as we can, we shelter them from any encounter with **the dark side of life**, instead encouraging them to believe that the world at large is like a magnified version of the family home. Out there a loving Heavenly Father watches over all his children to ensure that none of them comes to any serious harm. Out there all things are bright and beautiful, because the Lord God made them all.

Once inculcated, the myth of a loving Heavenly Father and his moral providence creates expectations which may have an important influence on our later social thinking. The optimistic expectations reflect deeply held convictions about the way the world ought to be, and the way that our everyday social life ought to run. We may well conclude that we ought to try to build a world that *looks as if* it has been made and is now watched over by a loving Heavenly Father. But of course the expectation – the *'realist'* expectation – that this will turn out to be the way the world already really *is*, is sure to be disappointed as the child moves on to secondary school, where a background religious view of the world is no longer taken for granted. The child learns that the scientific view of how the world works is value-neutral, and has been since the seventeenth century. In addition, it soon becomes obvious to everyone that people's liability to suffer major accidents and severe illness is largely statistical. It is a matter of 'luck', and not in proportion to their merits or demerits.

So far, so obvious: people complain that **Life is not fair** because the world of their childhood was so unnaturally cosy and protected, and because they were taught to believe in a wise and good moral Providence controlling all events. When the world turns out to be a somewhat colder place than they were led to expect, they feel let down. I well remember that when David Attenborough's big television series *Life on Earth* was first being broadcast, I received many letters of complaint from distressed adult members of the public who had been horrified to learn – apparently, for the first time – how cruelly competitive the world of animals is. How could God allow such things to happen?, they asked.

Well, my correspondents were grown up and should have known better. But in any case, it is worth asking whether we actually *want* a world in which life is fair, and all people meet during their lifetimes with just the fates they deserve. Imagine that God runs the world exactly in accordance with the prescriptions of the simplest and strictest small-town morality. For example, every practising male homosexual gets HIV, and only they get it. The good people live long and become rich, whereas the bad people soon come to a sticky end. All of them, without exception. If you are suddenly diagnosed as suffering from a terminal illness, you can infer that God is wrathful toward you and you are heading for damnation, a fate which you may be able to avert by sufficiently full acts of confession, contrition and repentance at this late stage. Think through in detail exactly what it would be like to inhabit a world in which the way things go in life is exactly in accordance with the way they ought to go – where, in Kantian terms, Nature and Morality are fully harmonized. Everyone promptly gets just what he or she deserves.

Nobody feels sorry for the sick or unfortunate, because they clearly must deserve their fate. The saints rule in a world where the good people are firmly in the saddle, and the bad ones are firmly underfoot. Duty and the purest self-interest exactly coincide. The ruling class would be superbly, and justly, *self-righteous* to the highest degree.

It sounds an utterly repulsive (and depressingly familiar) world. Is not this the way many rich people still claim to think the world is, or should be? Surely, anyone with any talent or spirit must promptly rebel or look for a way to escape from it.

We began with the common complaint that **life's not fair**; that **there's no justice in life**. I have argued that this reflects unjustified expectations implanted in us during our childhood, the resultant notion that we are *entitled* to expect life to be like that, and our shock when we learn that it is not so.

I reply to the initial complaint by elaborating the title of chapter 4, above: just as life exceeds and laughs at all our faiths and ideologies, so it also exceeds and mocks all our moral theories. Indeed, of our received moral theories only utilitarianism is moderately rational and humane. The rest are absurd, and it is good to see philosophers increasingly inclined to say so.[2] Bernard Williams in particular rejects what he calls 'the morality system', meaning the 'deontological' type of ethical theory, presented in its purest form by Kant, and revolving around ideas of moral law, universalizability, categorical obligation, duty, principle, conscience, the freedom of the will, guilt, blame and desert. This sort of ethic – theological ethics *minus* God – abstracts, rationalizes and makes an autonomous system out of everything that is most inhuman and terrifyingly oppressive in realistic theism. Bernard Williams quite rightly makes sharp philosophical criticisms of it all, and I have added that nobody should wish we had a world run like that. We should not wish to live under a theological dictatorship of the righteous, whether of the Islamic or of the Reformed Protestant type. In practice the rule of the righteous is the worst of all forms of tyranny.

We should instead simply prefer life as it is, excessive, exuberant, sometimes casually cruel and sometimes casually glorious. We should give up the problem of evil, and stop complaining that things are not other than they are. In fact, we should stop complaining altogether. Given life's contingency, it is only to be expected that there will be severe ups and downs. By many of the stock phrases they use, people show that they fully understand the position: **I'll take it as it comes**, they say, **We must learn to take the rough with the smooth**. Or, most simply of all, **That's the way it goes**, or **That's life**.

Chapter 13

That's Life

When we saw ourselves as living in a cosmos, people often felt that the cosmos somehow had a duty to be *just* in its treatment of individuals – the main reason for this being that people saw the cosmos as being in every way well-ordered and pervaded by reason. Either it was immanently rational, or it was the work of a rational Creator. If it was well-ordered, it was presumably *balanced*; and if it was balanced, it was presumably *just*.

Nowadays we tend to start not from the cosmos, but from ourselves, and for most of the time see ourselves as living beings, each with a part in life and each with a personal life to live. Our thinking has tended to become very life-centred; and when we are looking at things from the point of view of life, we are pretty sure that **life is not fair**. As I have been suggesting, we make the point in a variety of ways, referring variously to **things, it, it all** – and sometimes even **God**, for if one of our enemies gets his well-deserved comeuppance, we are apt to smile with satisfaction, and say that **There is a God, after all**!

We do not normally expect life to be fair. On the contrary, we seem to expect life to behave like a contrary young person, or a member of the opposite sex who is determinedly idiosyncratic. She declines to be managed, or to conform to our expectations. She's set upon being whimsical, having her own way, making her point. She is going to be very awkward in order to make sure that we don't take her for granted. We grunt, and you say 'Typical!'. In the case of life, our tone is probably just a little more resigned: **That's life!**, we say: **that's how it is, that's the way it goes,** for as we know **life's like that.** It is notable that this personifying of life as a capricious woman is very close to the way we speak of **Lady Luck,** or of success as **the bitch-goddess** (compare **life's a bitch!**). Once again, the idioms point out how very difficult it sometimes is to get – and to keep – our life under control. The cosmos-centred type of thinking that largely prevailed in the early modern West and during the Enlightenment put knowledge first, and was dominated by spatial metaphors. The world was seen as orderly, classifiable: everything could be *tabulated,* just as fruiterers and greengrocers lay out their produce before us in a neat rectangular grid of boxes on a tilted table. Life-centred thinking is very different. It sees the world in terms of life stories, and always has the effect of emphasizing the way a group of people, such as your contemporaries at school, start off pretty much on a level but end up a few decades later in wildly different places. Why are people's fates in life so extraordinarily diverse? Thirty years ago none of us had an inkling of what awaited us. We never dreamt that it would all turn out like this. What happened to us? We'll never know.

It is because our fates in life are so varied and seemingly unpredictable that life-centred thinking attends so much to unique individual stories. In life, everything is unique. Its typical media are the novel, biography, drama and film, and we are happy to formulate our wisdom of life on the basis of single cases, closely examined. It seems to be sufficient that the single case appealed to has a certain mythic quality: it reminds us of many other cases and somehow *appeals* to people.

Cosmos-centred thinking works quite differently. It is scientific: it is interested in making and justifying generalizations, and in making and testing theories. It assumes that everything around us is a member of many classes of things that are alike in this or that respect, and it assumes that events happen in accordance with general rules. Cosmos-centred thinking insists that **everything is under control**, and does not want to hear about the excessive or the irrational; whereas life-centred thinking recognizes life's excessiveness, unmanageability, unpredictability and sheer arbitrariness. In an earlier piece of writing I followed D.H. Lawrence in pointing out that much of our talk about life is modelled on older ways of speaking about God: we should **love life, commit ourselves to life, trust life** and **have faith in life,** because **life is sacred, life calls us, life teaches us,** and will **carry us into the future that it holds**

for us. We should never **despair of life**, nor **blaspheme against life** – and so on. But if life (which is indeed usually feminine) is a goddess, then she is like fortune – a troublesome, capricious goddess, and the sort of figure who appears in many mythologies as a whimsical, embarrassing troublemaker among the gods. And when we personify life as an awkward customer, a partner to whom we are uneasily yoked, then perhaps we are thinking of life as finite, and not as a divinity after all.

No, not quite that. What happens is that the wild excessiveness and capriciousness that we attribute to life is reflected in the sheer number, variety and *ribaldry* of our life idioms. Sometimes we are realists about life, and speak of it as a force or vitalizing energy that springs up in us or circulates among us. Sometimes we speak of an **appetite for life**, as if we attach ourselves to it and feed upon it. At other times we are non-realists, and insist that life is what we make it. At still other times we are semirealists who picture life as a semi-independent and comically capricious being that accompanies us, calls us, provokes us, and at times pulls against us as if it had a mind of its own. I have suggested that life, as the mocking, provocative Other that piques us and needles us, may readily be pictured as one's sexual partner; but we may equally find life personified in our own sexuality (or in the case of a young man, his penis, which keeps on piping up, provoking him, demanding to be noticed, and generally wanting to embarrass him and to have its say).

It seems that in each of us human beings there is a strong propensity to speak of oneself as two. I am always the straight man, and the Other with whom I am in dialogue is always the funny man. The Other may be my penis, or my sexuality, or my unconscious, or some *alter ego* or inner voice, or my manservant, or my sexual partner, or simply – and summing it all up – life, or It All, or Things, or Luck, or Fate, or God. It is a measure of the general excessiveness of life that the Other upon whom I tend to project my sense of the absurdity and the mysteriousness of the human condition can be so very variously pictured. **That's life!**

Do I wish that this absurd situation could be simplified and made more manageable? I don't think so. It is a large part of the puzzle of life that although life is so excessive and irrational, I somehow can't seem to be able to bring myself to wish that in any way things were any different.

Chapter 14

Optimism and Pessimism about Life

It is often said of the Romantic movement that it was always drawn to excess. Since it reacted against the Classical discipline of conventions and limits, by overflowing boundaries and seeking out extremes of every kind, we are not surprised that with the Romantics thinking first became life-centred in a big way. (Of course, life itself has always tended to every sort of extremity.) And it was in the same period, around 1820 or so, that the contrast between optimism and pessimism, as contrasting temperaments and attitudes to life much discussed by Schopenhauer, first became a highly prominent and appealing matter. It is an intellectual puzzle. After all, life is tumultuous and excessive in every way. It encompasses all the opposites, it cannot be systematized. So how does it come about that a rational person's overall attitude to life may be either as relentlessly sour and pessimistic as Schopenhauer's, or as cheery and good-humoured as William James's?[1] Both were notable thinkers, and the basic facts of life were surely the same for both. So why the huge difference between them, and what does it tell us?

Obviously four possibilities exist: 1. Schopenhauerian pessimism and resignation is alone rational; 2. Jamesian optimism is the most rational view of life and policy for living; 3. Because life contains all the opposites, there is enough evidence around for *both* optimism and pessimism to be defensible as rational outlooks and policies for living; and finally 4. *Neither* optimism nor pessimism is rational. On this last view optimists are merely lucky people who were born with a talent for looking on the bright side, enjoying life and making the best of things, whereas pessimists like Schopenhauer are unlucky people, miserable old curmudgeons. It was very unfortunate for Schopenhauer that he could never get on with his rather cold and frivolous mother, and ended up a heterosexual misogynist. But the issue between him and William James is not one that can be negotiated by reason.

We have sketched four possibilities, but I think we already suspect that they may be reducible to a smaller number. For one thing, the fourth statement suggests that the difference between optimists and pessimists is merely a difference of temperament – perhaps a difference in initial endowment or in the way we've been moulded by our upbringing. Either way, the presumption is that none of us can do much about the temperament that he is now stuck with. In this case the difference between optimists and pessimists may be a matter for empirical psychology to discuss, but it is not of any special philosophical interest. For some people the glass will always be half full, and for other people the same glass will always be half empty, and that is that.

We can also note right away that William James's position combines the second and third options. He allows that there is enough evidence around to permit both optimists and the pessimists to construct cases for their own point of view. But, he also insists that 'faith in a fact can help to create the fact': a person who has self-belief will tend to do better in life than a person who entirely lacks confidence, and students whose teachers think highly of them tend to perform better than they would if their teachers thought poorly of them. Thus both optimism and pessimism tend to be self-confirming, and the optimist will eventually find himself living in a much happier world than that inhabited by the pessimist. Optimism thus tends to justify itself, and in the end only the second position remains. Optimism turns out to be the only truly rational policy: has not America's traditional liberality and optimism led to American world hegemony, and has not the more pessimistic and sceptical outlook of many Europeans functioned as an ideology of Europe's slow relative decline?

The case for something like William James's outlook will be complete if it turns out to be true that we can teach optimism and train people to enjoy life. That way, we would 'prove' (i.e. test out) optimism by practising it. But as yet we have not done very much in this direction.

Since Hellenistic times the pessimists have had it almost all their own way. Western culture has taken a predominantly very negative view of human nature, the body, the passions, the senses and in general of the possibilities for human happiness and fulfillment in this life. The life of a sinner like you was not meant to be enjoyed, but to be spent in virtuous hard work. Education (like life itself) had a predominantly disciplinary purpose; and even to this day all governments and most voters see education as training in employable skills and social conformity. A more humane educational theory begins in the West with writers like Rabelais, Montaigne, and Locke, and develops rapidly after Rousseau and Schiller.[2] Today we can point to a number of real achievements. We are much more aware of the need to promote children's good health, and nowadays particularly their *mental* health. We give much better opportunities to the handicapped. Today at least some education is generally available in a number of areas which in the past were badly neglected, such as sport, music and sex. But in other areas, and above all in what Michel Foucault called 'the care of the self',[3] we remain very negligent. Modern Western societies have had enormous success in making people's lives longer, healthier and more prosperous, but we are not at all good at teaching and practising the arts of personal happiness. We are not the people we should be, and we are not as happy as we should be.

For a very long period we took a highly pessimistic view about human nature and about our chances of earthly happiness. Our best and indeed our *only* viable option was to spend the whole of this life in a state of probation, disciplining ourselves and cultivating the virtues. It is not surprising that when people thought in those terms the social order and morality became almost military by today's standards. During this life we were *in via*, on the road, and the Church was 'militant'. Now was not the time for rest and sensuous indulgence: in this life, reason and the will must rule the body and the passions.

Today that old outlook has passed away. The names of Marx and Darwin will briefly recall the severe political and biological criticisms that have been levelled against it, not to mention the fact that we all of us know in our hearts that talk of 'life after death' must now be given up. But unfortunately, enough of the old outlook survives to produce harmful effects on morality and on people's ability to enjoy life. 'Morality' is still *preached downwards* with the aim of keeping the young and the poor in order; 'morality' too often takes the form of a repressive and sadistic moral*ism*; 'morality' too often sets people at odds with their own bodies and their own emotions; and finally the vocabulary of morality (the moral law, obligation, principle, the will, conscience, the right, duty) is passing out of daily use because people frankly and cordially dislike it. And they are right. It is high time we learned to be less hard on ourselves and on each other; it is high time we learned how to love this life and live it well. It's all we'll ever have.

Chapter 15

The Meaning of Life

Philosophers hate the phrase '**the meaning of life**', and would never use it voluntarily – unless, perhaps, they could be allowed to repunctuate it as 'the meaning of "life" ', i.e., the *word* 'life'. They reckon that only words have meaning. They hate the idea of 'meaning' as a highly-desirable spiritual stuff that we are all searching for. So throughout the present discussion we are attempting to keep within language and avoid superstition by starting each section with stock phrases, and by always steering close to the idiomatic uses of the word 'life' in current speech. There is indeed much to be said for the view that in talking about 'meaning' we should confine ourselves to *linguistic* meaning. Talk of some extra-linguistic 'meaning of life' – perhaps a lofty Purpose, behind the scenes – sounds all too like talk of some hidden spiritual order behind appearances that satisfies the soul and explains everything. But that realist notion of meaning is a form of platonism, and must be avoided.

Nevertheless, I have to admit that ordinary language itself recognizes a sense in which seemingly extra-linguistic goings-on do have meanings – ordinary human meanings. Suppose someone is found acting suspiciously, and the voice of authority asks accusingly, 'Kindly explain what you are up to. **What is the meaning of this**?' What is being demanded? The answer is obvious: a good explanation. The action or event that has aroused suspicion needs to be put in the context of a credible story about how some quite innocent purpose is being fulfilled in an entirely innocent way. If the suspect can produce, on the spot, a plausible story about what he is up to, and if (better still) he can produce some corroborative evidence to show that his story is indeed much the likeliest explanation of what is going on, then he will probably get away with it.

A meaning, in this sense, is a narrative explanation. The meaning of some odd, anomalous event or state of affairs is shown by telling a story about the fulfillment of some human purpose to which this event or state of affairs contributes. We may then be able to think of some way of checking out the story – and now we are reminded that all these things are done in the classical detective story. The odd, anomalous events or states of affairs are *clues*. They seem to be relevant to the crime that is under investigation, and the detective looks for *narrative hypotheses* that will both account for the clues and indicate how and by whom the crime was committed. Then the detective looks for further evidence or tries to contrive a test that will confirm or refute the various available hypotheses. Thus the classical detective story exemplifies the way we get our bearings as persons in the human world by spotting significant details, generating narrative hypotheses and checking them out. Thus we work out what is going on – i.e., what other people in our immediate vicinity are up to – and to do it we must make informal use of a very large body of knowledge of contemporary life and manners; knowledge about how people 'tick', their motives, their typical patterns of behaviour, and so on. It is a kind of thinking in which women need to be not merely as accomplished as men, but much more so. Look at the skill with which Jane Austen has managed to hint to the reader that Mr. Elton is going to propose, not to young Harriet Smith, but to the over-manipulative matchmaker Emma Woodhouse.[1] We guess what's coming, but, clever though she is, Emma does not, and we are amused by her indignation and discomfiture. She is mortified, because in such matters a woman normally takes great pride in being able to rely upon the superiority of her own antennae. She knows exactly what to expect, because she's smarter than a man: it has to be so. But Emma has been blinded by her own vanity and manipulativeness, and it's no wonder that she feels a fool. A woman should never allow herself to be caught out like that.

All of this shows that in a certain sense there is a great deal of 'meaning' and reading of meanings in our life; but it is all piecemeal, it's all human, and the readings are all narratives about *human* motivations and intentions, and their varied expressions in human behaviour. Of course people used to make the analogous claim that in historical events they could find clues on the basis of which they could construct large-scale narratives about the fulfillment of *divine* purposes. Thus in the seventeenth century the burning down of Old St Paul's could be read as the wrath of God at the effeminacy of the current fashions in men's clothes; in the eighteenth century the Lisbon Earthquake could be seen as God's verdict on the state of religion in that city – some saying that God favoured Protestantism, and others that for God, Lisbon was not nearly Catholic enough; in the nineteenth century a current outbreak of the cattle plague (foot and mouth disease) in England could be understood as an admonition to repentance; and even in the late twentieth century the fire that damaged one of the transepts of York Minster just before his consecration was directly connected with the reported views of the new Bishop of Durham on the virgin birth. All of this, of course, is nothing but a catalogue of human folly. If by 'the meaning of life' we mean some large-scale narrative about the progressive fulfillment in history of a great suprahuman purpose, a story to which we have in certain historical events various keys, clues and pointers, then there is no such thing as the meaning of life. For many people, to believe that **our life has meaning** is to believe that everything is 'meant' – i.e., **happens for a purpose:** every event has been pre-ordained to contribute towards the realization of one grand design. But nowadays it seems that there is a lot of randomness in the way things go: whether or not a particular event occurs is a matter of probability. Hence we cannot hold that all of cosmic history is subsumable under a single great Story of Fall and Redemption. Indeed, our language and our world don't permit us to see or tell any such story.

The proof, very briefly, is this. As Wittgenstein remarks, 'The world and life are one'.[2] *We* invented language, and the only world that our language gives us is our human life world. Within the human life world the only meanings we can recognize and tell verifiable stories about are *human* meanings, that is, events and states of affairs through which *human beings* are busily expressing themselves, pursuing their goals and so on. There are in effect no meanings but human meanings, and we can have no rational basis for claiming to detect signs of the purposes and the activity of invisible *non-human* agencies. Our language simply does not and cannot give us the ability to tell rational, certifiable tales about the doings of any such beings. So we would do well to forget all about the meaning of life.

Further, when we turn our human life world into the world of natural science by eliminating all talk about intentions and purposes, what's left is a world without any immanent purposiveness at all, a world describable entirely in terms of efficient causes, probabilities, mechanism, and randomness. And this rigorously 'meaningless' way of describing the world has for centuries been spectacularly successful. Indeed, it has changed everything. Therefore it makes sense to presume that although human beings are evidently able to inject 'meaning' into life (by positing, pursuing, and attaining goals for themselves) there is no given or ready-made 'meaning of life' whatever. I may well inject religious meaning into my own life, but I will not find it laid on for me. We ought therefore to give up describing ourselves as 'seekers', people who journey in search of religious meaning or truth. The metaphor is radically misleading. In fact, if you haven't already got it inside you, you'll never find it in the world around you, however hard you look.

One other use of the phrase, 'the meaning of life', deserves to be mentioned, if only because at the time of writing it is the one most frequently encountered. Evangelical Christians use the phrase as bait. 'Alpha Course' discussions are currently advertised as providing 'an opportunity to explore the meaning of life', and Evangelicals will sometimes tell you: 'I believe that life has meaning', in the hope that you will be puzzled or piqued enough to ask them to tell you what they have in mind. If you do, they will declare their faith: they have found a way to live meaningful lives in the service of God and in the confident hope of Heaven. If you share their faith you will know that your own life is meaningful, and if you don't, then you won't. Life is considered meaningful if and only if it is spent in pursuit of a great promised *telos*, or Goal, and the Christian version of this idea is the true one.

I agree that it is good to have a vocation, in the sense of a cause or value to which one's life has been voluntarily dedicated. I have known and admired many people whose lives have been dedicated in this way to scientific research, to thought, to art, to love or to philanthropic work. But the use of the word 'meaning' in such a connection sounds muddled, and we should disregard the Evangelical belief that unless we share their faith our lives are empty and aimless.

Life Cycle

An unlooked-for consequence of the turn to life in modern Western thought has been that for most ordinary people biological or 'family' relationships have become more important and more constitutive of our very identity than any others.

An example of this is the urgency with which people born as a result of artificial insemination by donor (AID) claim a legal right to know the identity of their biological fathers. Until I know this, they say, 'I don't know who I am' – showing that they hold a modern form of traducianism, the theory that a person's soul or 'identity' is formed from material contributions by each of the two parents. In effect, I *am* my genetic endowment, and the genes from my biological parents do virtually everything to make me myself. Cultural influences upon the formation of the personality are evidently considered comparatively insignificant.

That is no doubt why, from the instant of death, the family nowadays effectively claims property in the corpse – all of it, including organs retained by the pathologist after a post-mortem. For the same reason, the family normally seeks to control what is said at the funeral and the memorial service, and death notices and the headstone commonly omit the profession and the social standing of the deceased. Instead only close family relationships are mentioned, as if they alone matter.

The overriding importance of family is also shown by the lengths to which people will go in support of a family member who in their perception has been maligned or wronged. People are now willing to burst into a school and assault a teacher who has attempted to discipline their child. They will campaign for decades to 'clear the name' of a relative who has been convicted by a court of law, or found grossly negligent by a court of enquiry. They are still campaigning for posthumous pardons for young soldiers who were executed for cowardice in the face of the enemy during the First World War. In such cases people show little regard for facts or evidence: they declare that they just 'know' that their kinsman was innocent, and announce their intention to go on 'fighting' for 'justice' until their demands are met in full. Quite frequently, they win.

All these are examples of a certain privatisation of life that has become more marked in the age of the mobile phone. People's important relationships with their fellowhumans are effectively confined to a very small group of intimates and family members. They may as a result have lost the sense of how to behave *in public*. Often, they react to economic and cultural globalisation by becoming extremely ethnocentric, and perhaps by reviving the old notion of a nation as a group of kinsfolk – a collection of descent groups linked by frequent intermarriage with each other.

Thus the turn to life in modern thought has had an unanticipated consequence: it has helped to revive the old and primitive ethics and politics of 'blood' – now redescribed as 'genes'. It has also made us much more aware of **the human life cycle**, and of the point in it that one has personally reached. The cultural events that are variously described as the end of the belief in progress, or 'the End of History' are tending to bring about the decline of linear, historical time and the return of cyclical, biological time.

Our experience of 'the human life cycle' and 'cyclical time' is rather novel, however, because the huge and still growing extension of the normal human **lifespan** means that we can expect to live for almost three generations – that is, for three turns of **the wheel of life**. Earlier ages were not very explicit on this point, and usually talked as if they supposed that **you live only once** and therefore there is only one turn of the wheel in the average human lifetime. Not so: today it is common for us to be acutely aware of the extent to which, in our thirties and during the second turn of the wheel, we are repeating our parents' marriage and our own upbringing. And then again when we become grandparents and the wheel turns for the third time, we are aware of being some-what detached: we have become observers of the continuity of life and cultural tradition. Earlier generations were not, I think, as vividly aware as we are of how much we *repeat* and are ourselves *repeated*; and this rather novel *multiple* experience of the human **life cycle** undoubtedly underlies and affects a great deal of our thinking and activity nowadays.

In the past, people's sense of the worthwhileness of life was often sustained by other-worldly religious beliefs and hopes, or by optimistic hopes for the future liberation of humanity. Today, neither supernatural faith nor the belief in progress is what it was. Instead, I suggest, many of us are finding a Proustian comfort in the regaining of lost time as the wheel turns and turns again, and we have repeated experiences of *déjà vu* in the course of the human life cycle.

Chapter 17

Life Stories

That's the story of my life, people exclaim when they hear a piece of narrative that echoes their own experience – and I suddenly recognize that in this remark *the way things have gone for me* has been blurred together with *a narrative account of the way things have gone for me*. It seems that I do not distinguish between the world and language, my life and the story of my life. The two are intertwined. In the same way, the term **a life** means both one person's lived span of life *and* a written biography, and 'history' means *not only* the occurrence of a long chain of public events, *but also* historiography, the work of producing written records of those events, *and* the consensus story that 'the history books' eventually settle upon.

Everywhere in our language, words and the world are already interwoven; they cannot be clearly separated or even distinguished from each other. By telling our stories about it we have *fixed* the world – that is, that we have made the world apprehensible, intelligible, discussible and, in a word, *public property*. Old-fashioned realism – or, if you prefer, *representationalism* – can still sometimes mislead people into supposing that we are here talking about two different things: the world which exists out there, determinate and independent of us, and our representation of the world in language. And sometimes it is said that the linguistic representation corresponds more or less closely to 'the facts' of the case. But that's not how it is at all. On the contrary, there is only one thing here, namely, a world that is always already formed completely by language. And if you doubt me, then think about life, life-stories, biography and history. Even as they were taking place, the original events were already entwined with stories that were shaping them, and were accompanied by their agents' running commentary upon them. Think about a journalist working on what journalists call **a story**: What's she doing? Is she investigating a chain of events, or is she building up a narrative? Which did the editor who gave her the job have in mind – the chain of events, or the story? The two are always interwoven. As she works on the story, checking details, gathering evidence and so on, the narrative she feels able to write gets longer, more complex, and better founded, and either more or less like what her editor originally had in mind for her to come up with. His long experience made him suspect that if she looked into the story, she might be able to make something interesting out of it. So he put her on the job. And she knows what kind of thing he wants. So she works on the story. But of course she's not merely writing fiction in order to please her boss. On the contrary, both she and her editor know perfectly well that the story has got to **stand up**. That is, the additional evidence, the background and the subplots must *justify* her writing the elaborated story with the plot that her editor wants. I am not suggesting for a moment that truth is irrelevant to journalists. But I *am* pointing out that the whole enquiry began with a veteran editor's nose for a story. The journalist is a wordsmith. She gathers material and works up her narrative. Her task is to produce both a story **that stands up**, and also one that her editor wants. The story must be interesting, and **in the public interest**. It must **stick**, and if it's good it'll **run and run**, and of course the editor will **stand by it**.

Newspapers don't just gather cold extra-linguistic facts about the world and publish them duly coded into language. No, they do much more than that. They tell *stories*. The whole human life world, and especially the political world, is a great arena in which a host of stories jostle and compete. The loudest voices – that is, the voices of politicians, journalists and other popular leaders – tell big stories, stories that reflect and press us to share their values, their interpretations of events, and their view of the world. In a word, amongst the multitude of stories jostling within us and around us, there is a perpetual struggle for dominance. Politicians are leading figures in that struggle, and so are journalists; so are scientists nowadays, and so are a few leading religious figures.

Those who tell the dominant stories are the people who have *power*, because it is they who determine what counts as truth, reality, history — in a word, the way things are.

How, you may well ask, does all this work out within the individual self? My self is an anthology of stories, running in my head, that reflect various influences upon me and impulses within me. Our myriad stories show up in our fantasies about where we'd like to get to in ten years' time, and about the kind of person we'd like then to have become: I **can see myself as...**, we sometimes say. But now a puzzle arises that I don't immediately know how to resolve: should I attempt to make of myself a story-monarchy, or should I be content to remain a story-democracy?

By *becoming a story-monarchy* I mean unifying myself and my activities under the rule of a single master narrative about how I am journeying towards and hoping to achieve the chief end or goal of my life. A powerful tradition inherited from antiquity, and quite naturally pre-empted by religion, says that we ought to become unified selves. Every different bit of ourselves and our lives ought to be arranged and *organized*, so that we pursue as efficiently as possible the highest good (*summum bonum*) for which we humans were created. Even Nietzsche, who is ordinarily such a radical critic of his own tradition, doesn't question this one: he thinks we should forge unified (sovereign, creative) selves out of the miscellany of sometimes warring impulses that we have grown up with. Yes, even Nietzsche believes in self-discipline and self-forging. He wants to be unified.

But I am not sure that I do. Tradition tells me that I ought to prioritize all the great concerns of my life in their correct order of value; I must get myself really clear about the ultimate and the proximate, the intrinsic and the instrumental, the long-term and the short-term. I must rank all my varied loves in a proper *ordo amoris*, as Augustine calls it. That means I've got to think really carefully about what my life has all along been about — and also, *should* have been about. 'The Good is that at which all things aim', goes Aristotle's maxim: so what has been the supreme concern of my own life, around which I ought by now to have got my life properly organized? Religion, philosophy, love, writing, visual joy (in painting, butterflies, landscapes...), my pupils, art...? What have I cared about most of all, what indeed *should* I have cared about most, and how am I going to slot all the other concerns into their properly subordinate positions?

I can't do it. I don't think we *are* real *monarchists* about the self and 'the spiritual life', any longer. I think we are increasingly attracted to at least a measure of pluralism about stories, about values and about life aims. Thus the self is becoming somewhat plural.

We need to be careful about what we do and do not mean to say at this point. The main Western tradition since Parmenides and Plato has believed very strongly that the whole world of value is metaphysically unified in the Good, or the One, or God, and that we need to become unified selves living a life that is directed in a rational way towards the attainment of our One Last End, the *telos* or goal of human existence. Until quite recently, philosophers either accepted this maxim or at least hesitated openly to reject it. One should be, or try to become, a self-consistent unified self, and one's ethic should be rational – i.e., worked up into a single system. Very recently, however, Isaiah Berlin has provided an example of a major philosopher who urges us to admit openly that the world of value cannot be fully systematized. We do find ourselves owing allegiances we cannot renounce to a range of distinct values that are sometimes in conflict with each other. Nor is this surprising, because once the old metaphysics has been lost, nothing guarantees the ultimate unity of all value.

I have been in or very close to this position for many years. Life itself is endless, shapeless and excessive in every direction, and it includes all the moralities and theories of value. The world of value is coextensive with the life world. Therefore, if there cannot be a unified systematic philosophy of *life*, there cannot be a unified systematic philosophy of *value* either. Nor can there be a perfect life. And this is especially true of well-informed late modern people, who cannot help but be acutely aware of cultural, religious, and ethical pluralism. So, if I ask myself 'What has been the great love of my life?', I cannot give a sufficiently clearcut answer to satisfy traditionalists. I can only point to an obvious cluster of obsessions. I don't *want* to get more rigorously unified than that. I don't *want* to be a strong monarchist, a single-issue person whose whole life is tightly focussed on the pursuit of one supreme goal. My cluster of obsessions allows me to vary the emphasis and shift the focus a little as time goes by, and I am glad of that little bit of freedom to change direction.

Religious conservatism is often associated with nostalgia for a simpler age, when life was dominated by the absolute monarchy of a single great master narrative. But I don't want that degree of 'focus'. It's a kind of cosmic careerism, and is a mistake. In the non-realist universe it is not appropriate to be fixated: one should be free.

*   *   *   *   *

In reaching this conclusion I have found an answer to a question that has long troubled me. Should we try to leave behind us a completed life story that is like a work of art? Lord Nelson is the best example of someone who planned and successfully created his own myth. Should we emulate his example? Consciously or unconsciously, Nelson seems to have successfully chosen the time and the manner of his own death: but most of us will not have such a good opportunity as the one he saw and seized. We don't know exactly when we will die. And now to the difficult question: Ought I then to live in such a way that my life will be artistically rounded off and complete whether it ends in two months or in twenty years?

It is true that our religion always taught us to 'live each day as if thy last'. But do I really need to find a way of living such that each page of my life story is lived as if it will turn out to be the last? Surely, if I am ever to carry through any great enterprise that will take years to complete, I am going to have to forget about my mortality and cheerfully take the risk of leaving a big job unfinished. It is both futile and vainglorious to spend time trying to construct and leave behind us a neatly rounded-off personal myth. Nelson was his own spin-doctor and he managed it beautifully, but the very fact that we *know* that Nelson successfully organized his own posthumous cult should make anyone else who tries to do something similar feel rather silly.

That answers my question. Life is too big and varied and absurd and untidy for any of us to be able to create and control his or her own personal myth. We shouldn't worry about such things. They are all vanity. Nor should we expect to be able to totalize our own lives in one great mythic narrative, or to sell such a story to posterity. Through the influence of Plutarch and others, the West has made a little bit too much of biography.

Chapter 18

Life's a Walking Shadow

Life's but a walking shadow, a poor player
That struts and frets his hour upon the stage
And then is heard no more: it is a tale
Told by an idiot, full of sound and fury,
Signifying nothing.
Macbeth V.v

When Shakespeare, speaking through the mouth of one of his tragic heroes, has worked himself up into a nihilistic mood, he can sound unexpectedly dark and modern for his date. In view of what is shortly to happen to him, Macbeth certainly has every reason to take a dim view of 'life', but what he says here strikingly anticipates the tone of much later pessimists such as Schopenhauer and Sartre (and others too, perhaps, such as Kleist, Schubert, Hardy and Beckett). 'Life' is a transient scrap of theatre that locally and only briefly interrupts the larger cosmic silence; 'life' is a story that falters and disappoints, tailing off into inconsequential nonsense.

The image of life as a walking shadow looks back to Plato's Cave, and forwards to the cinema. It suggests flickering insubstantiality. And the implication, right through from Macbeth to Sartre, is that this is not how things should be: *we were led to expect otherwise*. We expected, we felt we had a right to expect, divine providence, or history, or progress, or something. We expected the course of events both in the world at large and in our own lives to run like a vast, coherent narrative in which one can discern a general drift of things, a great plan being gradually worked out, and events being orchestrated towards a final culmination or fulfillment when 'the earth shall be filled with the knowledge of the glory of the Lord, as the waters cover the sea'. In and through the way things go, we expected to be able to glimpse a consistent thread of purpose running and values being upheld. But we have been violently and cruelly disappointed, and we find ourselves left with a feeling of emptiness, coldness and barrenness, like the character in A.E. Housman's poem who feels 'alone and afraid / In a world I never made'.

In a word, what Shakespeare/Macbeth is talking about is the loss of belief in a moral Providence, a phenomenon that would eventually come to be called the Death of God. Even to this day, most people expect religion to give us the feeling that the course and the direction of our own lives is in harmony with, indeed is part of a larger cosmic purposiveness that is moving forward and will in the end prevail. There is a Power at work in the world that makes for righteousness and we can join forces with it. We want to feel part of something larger that will endure, because we want to feel that our life's work will not be at once and utterly lost when we die. We want to feel that we are contributing something to a cosmic enterprise that will continue after we are gone. But with the end of Communism, the end of belief in progress, and the end of belief in life after death, we appear to have lost all forms of the belief that whatever great cause we have served, or good we have done, or things we have loved, will be conserved. The loss of that unifying thread or stream running through everything seems to reduce the world to rubble, as people say.

There can be no doubt that many people, in the West at least, are haunted by the spectre of universal insignificance and oblivion. People approaching death regularly hint to me how much they are troubled by the thought that they, their world and everything they have cared about will very soon be forgotten forever. The same anxiety shows in the efforts of such senior philosophers as Charles Hartshorne, and scientists such as Barrow and Tipler, to defend the idea that we may be remembered – whether by God or by the supercomputers of the far future.[1]

The most important literary monument to this particular form of cosmic anxiety is Tennyson's *In Memoriam* (1850). It shows how closely the worry about cosmic meaning is linked with Christian spiritual individualism. If the unique individual human being can matter so much to us and be loved so intensely by us, then surely the universe has a positive *duty* to back us up and conserve that which is infinitely precious to us. For if it doesn't, if death really does have the last word, then our life and our mutual love are unendurably poignant and sad.

So there are people, and there have even been theologians,[2] who have argued that there has *got* to be personal immortality, because the alternative – the everlasting extinction and oblivion of ones whom we have loved more than life itself – is somehow unbearable. But, of course, if we were Buddhists we would not think this way at all. Buddhism *starts* by making it crystal clear that nothing is permanent, not even the self. Love and compassion for the fellow mortal are by no means absent from Buddhism, but in Buddhist culture preachers and poets do not make the Western mistake of promising to immortalize the beloved. Truly nothing is permanent, and we in the West might have saved ourselves a great deal of unhappiness if we had never got into the habit of trying to comfort people by making false promises to them.

So far in this section I have described a classic Western religious view of life (there is a moral Providence), and a classical Western atheist view of life (the Universe is non-moral and utterly indifferent to our fate). I have also briefly mentioned Buddhism. But now I want to describe the point of view which I have held for nearly twenty years and am defending once again in this book. It is different. It is not the same as any of the three just mentioned. It is very simple, but there is no doubt that people find it very hard to understand. I first encountered it, or something very close to it, in about 1983 when Michel Nedo explained to me his understanding of Wittgenstein's position: 'Wittgenstein was not a theist. Wittgenstein was not an atheist. Wittgenstein was not an agnostic.'[3] 'Very well: so what *did* he think?' Things are what they are ... quietism ... subtle positivism ... linguistic naturalism. Understand the idioms, see how the language works, that's all there is. *Really* all there is. It is odd that Wittgenstein's position has been explained so often and so clearly but *still* hasn't quite caught our imaginations.

My version of all this began in about 1985, the key words being 'anthropomonism' and 'outsidelessness'.[4] The first means: 'There's nothing radically non-human, and nothing alien. We ourselves developed **it all** – all our language, all our knowledge, our whole picture of the world, our entire way of life. We made the lot. So there's only *our world* and we ourselves who are parts of it.' The second key word means: 'There is no unseen metaphysical or supernatural order behind our world. But this doesn't mean that behind our world there is nothing, a void. It is not as if there is a horrid gap where there ought to be foundations, supports and backing. No. Nothing's missing, because our life world is simply outsideless. It has no outside. The question of whether it does or does not have some external support simply does not arise. For this subtle form of positivism, there's no metaphysical order; there is only the human world, the world of language. We are in a bubble we blew up ourselves and there is *only* the bubble – at least, so far as those inside it will ever be able to tell.

This philosophical position is described in my more recent writings as 'Empty radical humanism'. The word 'Empty' is capitalised by way of a reminder that it is being used in the Buddhist sense. We are talking about a thoroughly post-metaphysical outlook. There are no substances, or real essences, or spirits. There is only, and outsidelessly, the dance of signs and the world-bubble it conjures up. As we are the only makers of our world, we need to remind ourselves that we are also the only makers *of ourselves*. Once again, we have only our own language, and therefore only our world. We have no basis at all for talking about anything else, or indeed for supposing that there *is* anything else. We should stick *to* our language and our world because we are stuck *with* our language and our world – which are outsideless.

This 'Empty radical humanism' is wonderfully economical and liberating. It enables us to shake off forever every kind of superstition, and therewith every kind of undue self-concern. There is no real, objective and extra-human value, meaning or purposiveness out there. And there is nothing out there to be afraid of because everything that is 'out there', we put there. The fact that it was *we* alone who differentiated our language and our sense experience and who built our world picture, explains why in all ages the poets have seen the inner and outer worlds as images of each other, and have spoken of the world as macrocosm and the self as microcosm. It also explains the vogue on the battier fringes of science for something called 'the anthropic principle'. Why does the world seem to be so likely to have produced us? Because *we* produced *it*, of course! We, our language and our world, are perfect images of each other, adapted to each other, transparent to each other – *don't you see!* There's just the one continuum, and it is ours all through. So we can be completely free of the gloomy old atheist idea that the world is alien, cold, and indifferent to us. On the contrary, the world is ours; we made it. Haven't you ever noticed how beautifully the perceived world about you is adapted to the range and the capacities of your sense organs, and wondered how this can be so? Behind your way of seeing stretches a long cultural tradition, and the reason why the 'objective' world about you is so beautiful is that your eyes paint the picture they see. They cook and feast at once. Our eyes differentiate the world to use up all the colours we can see, all the detail and all the depth. The world *fills* our senses, sates them. Nor is there any problem of evil, for on my account we get and we have *exactly* the world we deserve. For the most part, it should be accepted as a package deal, like marriage. If there are respects in which we don't like it, we should acknowledge them and set about reshaping things, by redescribing them.

So is Macbeth right, and is our life a mere 'walking shadow', 'signifying nothing'? No, Macbeth's view is much too dark – too dark because Macbeth is a major villain who is heading rapidly for the fate he thoroughly deserves. For us, the world is phenomenal (sensuous, 'bright', transient), formed by our language, and thereby appropriated by us to ourselves and filled with value spread over everything by us. The world is our home, and if it is transient, so are we. We all of us, and everything else, are equally transient. The transience of all that we love is intensely poignant, but also extremely consciousness-raising. It makes us *aware* of earthly beauty and of love. I don't know how things could have been radically different, and therefore I must say 'Yes' to it all as it is. Bits of the world that I have myself shaped are ill-made, and I can try to remake them; but the general contingency and transience of all things should be simply accepted.

Living Well

Long ago, Greek philosophy drew a contrast between merely *living* and **living well** (*eu zen*[1]). The contrast was often made in order to introduce the subject of ethics: the argument ran that just as you need to learn a skill and practise it diligently in order to pursue each of the various arts and crafts, so there is also **an art of living** as such, which needs to be carefully studied and practised by us all if we are to live as well as humans should live. A moment's thought will add the important point that besides ethics, which is the theory of the good life, the art of living well must also include instruction in prudence, in practical wisdom, and in a wide range of social skills if it is to produce vigorous citizens and leaders.

In one way and another, the contrast between mere living and **living well**— excellent living, **good living**— is still being drawn today. But the modern idioms lay a great and rather novel emphasis on the need to **live life to the full**, talking about the personal satisfaction we enjoy when we are passionately engaged with life. For the Greeks, life was important only as a realm in which eternal ideal values could be briefly manifested in time. But for us, 'life' is much more than that.

For example, we may say of somebody who no longer enjoys his work that **he's going through the motions, but his heart isn't in it any**

more. Of such a person – and also of somebody whose life is hard and narrow, with little room for leisure or enjoyment – we may say that he's **merely existing; it's not really a life**. The desire for and enjoyment of life, which roughly equals what people currently call 'libido', is nowadays considered a necessity, and is spoken of in very strong language: consider the phrases **the joy of life, appetite for life, lust for life, zest for life, the spice of life, rage for life, life force** and so on. The phrases seem to link the life impulse very closely with the sex drive; thus in the film *D.O.A.* (1990) the young heroine says to her rather washed-up and gloomy college English professor: 'Life is here. Life is now. Take it!'. He treats this as a direct sexual invitation, and she shows no inclination to correct him.

Until you have seen this or done that, people say, **you haven't really lived**. As we suggested earlier, modern people have picked up something of the vitalism of Nietzsche and the generation of writers who followed him. It is of paramount importance, it is indeed something like a religious duty, that we should commit ourselves to our own lives; and this commitment is a commitment of the passions, of the 'heart'. A number of eighteenth and nineteenth-century writers, ranging from Boswell to Lautréamont, attempted in various ways to explore the limits of human experience, but what we are talking about now is something even more radical, of which D.H. Lawrence was perhaps the prophet, namely, a demand that we should give up the old moralities of self-mastery by rational control of the passions, and instead affirm our own biological makeup and become emotionally fully invested in our own living. And in this, Lawrence may perhaps be seen to radicalize Wordsworth's injunction that we should **live by the heart**. If we don't try to do this, then whatever else we may or may not succeed in doing, we have missed out on the one thing needful, the *unum necessarium*. After all, **life is for living**, as people say. **Live hard. Make the most of it while you have it**.

What the new ethic of **living life to the full** means in practice is neatly illustrated by the new sexual ethics. People now speak of **exploring their sexuality** in order to discover their own sexual orientation. And when they find that they are, for example, homosexual, then they immediately acknowledge a duty to **come out**, to make contact with **the gay scene**, to become part of **gay culture**, to join **gay pride** marches and so on. The impulse of this relatively new ethic is always towards open publication and uninhibited self-expression – the opposite of the old ethic still promulgated in some Christian quarters, which demands the right ordering and the control of the passions by the will, in obedience to the dictates of reason and of God's Word.

If you accept that we are social animals with highly developed powers of symbolic expression and communication, animals who have invented knowledge and consciousness and have built up a rich and complex world around ourselves – but nevertheless *mortal* animals who **only live once** – then you must accept right away that the new ethic is obviously right and will prevail. That is my own view, despite an occasional fit of nostalgia for the old world view that is now finally slipping away. I have held, and have taught, that at some time in our lives – usually, when we have reached the professional plateau – we should all of us try to come out into the open and say in full whatever we have in us to say. It is not enough to sail all one's life under borrowed colours and live by second-hand beliefs. We should all of us attempt the hard labour of finding out 'what I myself really think'. This is a much more difficult task than exploring one's sexuality, but we need to do it. And what is also difficult, we need to find some way of 'outing' or expressing ourselves. In this way we can each of us make a distinctive personal contribution, however small, to the human scene. At least that's one way of **living well**. It's the only one I know.

Life Has No Outside

I hope you noticed the bubble, and were piqued by it. It appeared on page 84: 'there is no metaphysical order: there is only the human world. We are in a bubble we blew up ourselves — and there is *only* the bubble, at least so far as those inside it can tell.'

By this I mean that the whole strange, even magical world of linguistic meaning is a world that we generated by developing our capacities for reciprocal sympathy, sociability, creating symbols, and following rules. Simply out of chatter we generated language, established values, built up our huge and elaborate knowledge systems and — strangest of all — we even generated our own consciousness, our own subjective life.

The bubble is unmoored, outsideless: as seen from inside it, there is no way out of it. Until about the time of Hume and Kant in the eighteenth century, most philosophers had wanted to find some sort of a priori or metaphysical backing for the various human cultural creations and capacities. Life inside the bubble seemed evidently to depend upon external support from a larger realm outside. Thus meaning was grounded in a noumenal or intelligible world of essences or real meanings 'out there'; human mental life was grounded in the larger mind of God, or of a world soul, or a spirit world; human ideas of truth were referred to and checked against the ready-made truths of a real created world out there; human values were grounded in religious law, or the will of God, and so on.

The intellectual revolution that took place during the eighteenth century came at a time when – and was able to happen because – the old metaphysical God was still in place anchoring the balloon, guaranteeing objective reality, truth, value, and so on. While everything was still being held in place in that way, the scholars of the Enlightenment set about rearranging it all around human beings by redescribing everything exclusively from the human point of view, and by determining what capacities had enabled us to build our world for ourselves and around ourselves. When this was all done, the old metaphysical order died because it was no longer within the range of our capacities. As Kant saw, our capacities were sufficient to build our world, but not to build or even to comprehend reality itself. So God died, the bubble was cut loose, and everything became free-floating. Therefore, the phrase 'life has no outside' is to be taken as meaning something like this: in the past we saw the whole of our human life activity as both needing and having external validation whether by tradition or by God. But all that is now at an end. As we now see it, we have no reason to think that anything quite independent of us guarantees the link between our thinking, our language, and an objective world out there. It is as if the whole human life world is like a great iridescent bubble – perhaps, as Shelley calls it, 'a dome of many-coloured glass'. [1] We are all inside it. It floats free. There is no view of it from the outside: there is no reality behind appearances. As the popular phrase has it, **What you see is what you get**. It is all there is. Indeed, so far as we can know, we are quite alone. It may be that dolphins have a language and a world of their own – but we'll never be able to decipher it, because the dolphins' form of life is too different from ours. In which case the situation is exactly symmetrical: their world is nothing to us, and our world is nothing to them. To them we are just animals, as they are just animals to us. But however that may be, we know only humanity, the human angle on everything, the human life world, and the great knowledge systems that humans have developed. And getting accustomed to this situation is our way of facing up to the old challenge: we must learn to accept contingency.

A consequence of the view of our human condition that I have just described is that it is much less easy than it used to be to draw clear lines between fact and fiction, and between what's real and what is 'merely' a communal dream. People are going to enjoy making rude comments about me on that account, but I am firmly unrepentant. Don't we know, isn't it obvious, that historians *both* try to be accurate *and* make up stories? And is it not also obvious that a big religious system looks like a communal dream to outsiders, but feels like plain fact to insiders? Nowadays the insiders themselves are often aware of the doubleness, and acute enough to become ironical and humorous about it. They recognize both the grandeur and the absurdity of modern post-metaphysical knowledge. It is worth adding that the paradox arises just as much in physics as it does in theology, but is less often perceived, because physics has become so central and dominant that it is hard for physicists not to become self-important realists about their own subject.

Now to take the argument one step further and return to the philosophy of life: how much does our life *matter*, how *important* is our life to each one of us, when we have fully understood the bubble? That is, when we have understood the sense in which our life has no outside; when we have grasped the implications of the fact that over the millennia we have informally evolved amongst ourselves the whole of our language, our form of life, our consciousness, our vision of the world – the *lot* – all of that precious, cerebral stuff, now seen to be the mere product of time and chance and the casual operation of secondary causes just as our own bodies are – when we have grasped all this and have understood how utterly transient and contingent is every bit of us and our life, then what does it all matter? Is our life infinitely serious or infinitely trivial, or both at once?

Clearly, both at once. The first writer, or at any rate the first important writer, to see that the religious view of life is humorous was Kierkegaard. Religion sees that our life is both infinitely serious (because everything is final, and everything happens only once) and utterly absurd (because everything is so ultralight, contingent, evanescent, and insecure). Life is a little like the mixed genres in film: comedy thriller, black comedy, tragi-comedy. Faith is a way of keeping steady, and affirming life in that absurdly mixed situation.

The insecurity of life is most marked at its two ends, the periods immediately after birth and before death. That is why, as one gets older, one becomes more sceptical of attempts to plan one's life as a big narrative of progressive betterment and movement towards a 'chief end of man'. One also becomes sceptical of attempts to sweeten and improve one's own disposition by following an ascetical discipline. The last period of our life is not the most readily plannable, nor the most sweet-tempered, nor even the most important stage of life to which everything else leads up. On the contrary, it is an irritable rearguard action against degenerative disease and other casual misfortunes. Even more then than in earlier years, we do well to turn religious attention towards the present moment, and learn to find the highest religious happiness in the most ordinary and everyday things.

Chapter 21

Life Drawing

There is a very striking and important use of the word 'life' in art as a mass noun,[1] roughly equivalent to 'nature', and signifying 'the empirical world'. It is found in phrases such as **life class**, **drawing from life** and the paradoxical **still life**, and it refers to an artistic practice generally said to have begun in the early Renaissance (though no doubt there are earlier instances of it). The artist derives his representation of the subject, not just from his own imagination, and not from the traditional rules for the depiction of each subject that usually guide religious art, but directly from personal observation. At one stage the artist brought his eye very close to an observation point rather like a rifle sight, and looked over it through a framed grid at the subject. The idea was not just to learn about perspective: still more important, one was striving to represent as accurately as possible the way the phenomenal world – the world of the senses – appears to the unaided human eye. It came to be believed that the best education for a young artist must involve attending **life classes**, at which the students set up their easels around a posing **life model** so as to practise close observation and drawing **from life**, under the guidance of a master.

It is hard to remember now just how revolutionary this practice originally was. The older practice might involve apprenticeship to a master, and learning to work in the style of his studio by copying him. One might work **from the Antique**, by sketching a plaster cast of a classical sculpture: but since classical sculpture was already highly idealized, **drawing from the Antique**, although it gave problem-free access to nude subjects, was far from genuine life drawing. But the fact is that for a long time artists had difficulty in overcoming public suspicions about their motives for wanting to break with traditional iconography and establish fresh personal styles based on direct observation of life. Even today the artist is still, in the popular iconography of the cartoonist, a middle-aged man of doubtful morals who wears French or Italian-looking clothes and paints naked women. And whether justified or not, this popular suspicion helped to ensure that the female nude long remained a relatively undeveloped subject in art. Only a very few major figures like Rembrandt could paint it really convincingly, largely because access to live models was not easy – unless, like Bonnard and Hopper and so many others, the artist was content to paint only his own wife throughout his career. The phrase **the naked truth** reminds us that **truth to life** remained in some ways a Holy Grail, an elusive ideal right up to the nineteenth century – and for someone like Lucian Freud, perhaps even to the present day. We are, after all, aware of the huge gap between what culture says women ought to look like and women's actual measurements.

We begin to see that the appeal to 'life' in art is both more complicated and more revolutionary than at first appears. Think of a late mediaeval Flemish altarpiece in which we see on the same canvas both images of angels and of Christ and Mary made in accordance with the traditional rules, and images of the patron and one or two other living persons that have been taken from life using the techniques introduced by Jan Van Eyck. The angels, Christ and Mary are universals, figures of timeless ideal beauty, always with perfectly regular, symmetrical features. One cannot imagine any of them ever being wrinkled, or a little stout, or bald. It is out of the question. Whereas the patron is quite often an elderly, wrinkled and rather self-important figure. He has paid to have his piety publicized, but I like him nonetheless, because he is a mortal and like me he looks it. He is part of the transient phenomenal world, whereas the angels, Christ and Mary belong to the unchanging eternal world. They are not individuals, and never were.

Because the altarpiece somewhat incongruously mixes two very different worlds, we see how revolutionary is the appeal to **life** in art. It reminds us that religion and culture have long told us not to trust our own senses or this world. We should be guided entirely by universal normative conceptions derived from an ideal, heavenly world. But now it is time to forget tradition and to make a fresh start on the basis of trust in the human point of view, our senses, and the finite particular things of this world.

This shows why the Victorians were right to regard the Renaissance, rather than the scientific revolution, as the true beginning of the modern world. For it was the artists' turn to life that started everything: the rejection of tradition; the turn to the human point of view, the senses, and this world; scientific observation of nature; along with individualism, critical thinking, and liberal democracy.

The artists can hardly have been unaware of how profoundly they were contradicting standard piety. Thomas à Kempis, for example, a devotional writer immensely popular with the laity for centuries, was active in the Netherlands in the early fifteenth century. He was contemporary with the brothers Van Eyck, must have heard of them, and may have met them. But in *The Imitation of Christ* his opening page plunges straight into a demand for rejection of 'all the folly and unreality of this world'.[2] 'Detach your heart', he says, 'from the love of things which can be seen … transfer all your affections to things which cannot be seen'.[3] The whole books seeks to make us 'feel hatred and loathing of the world'.[4] 'It is a wretched thing', says Thomas, 'to have to live on earth'[5] – and it is even more wretched to plough on through the pages of a writer who so hates life, hates the senses and hates the world. But that is how we used to think. My copy was a Confirmation present to me dated 1949. There was a time when I solemnly read this stuff. Not any more: I threw the book away on the day I wrote these words.

Chapter 22

Knock Hard: Life is Deaf

In *The New Religion of Life in Everyday Speech* I set out to show that, as belief in God has declined during the past forty years, so a great deal of the old god-language has been displaced onto life. That is why we now hear people say that **life is sacred**, that we should **love life, have faith in life, trust life, commit ourselves to life** and so on. I asked readers for more material – and a startling amount came in. I was struck by the persistence of certain metaphors, and the vividness with which life tends to be personified.

Thus in St John's Gospel (3:8) there is a familiar verse comparing the Spirit of God with the wind, which 'blows where it wills, and you hear the sound of it, but you do not know whence it comes or whither it goes' (RSV). A correspondent looked into one of the big computer databases which collects examples of current English, and found for me **the winds of life**, which mysteriously blow us this way or that. He also added to the numerous sayings that warn us not to be presumptuous, or to **tempt life**. The best of them said: **we don't own life – we don't even control life**.[2] Life, like God, may suddenly bring down the proud. We should remember that **nobody's bigger than life**, a phrase used by the film actor Elliot Gould – who himself experienced a severe reverse.[3]

The winds of life recycles a familiar metaphor. **Knock hard. Life is**

deaf is new; it is an artist's postcard from the early 1990s.[4] It pithily repeats both the message *and* the ironical humour of Jesus' Parable of the Importunate Widow.[5] Pray hard, nag at God: haven't you noticed that the determined, persistent people who refuse to give up tend eventually to get what they want? In saying this, of course, we both invoke and smile at the image of God/Life as idle or deaf.

So strong is the impulse to transfer god talk to life that in spite of my own insistence that life is excessive and includes both good and evil, blessing and misery, many people are still ready to speak moralistically of life as imposing **duties** or **commandments** upon us. Thus, in the British film *The Night My Number Came Up* (1955) scripted by the playwright R.C. Sherriff, I have noted **That's our duty to life – to live it to the utmost**. And Nietzsche, despite his vehement atheism and love of freedom, had a very strong sense of being *bound* to a sacred vocation:

> Life has proposed my duty to me with the terrible condition
> that I should fulfill that duty in solitude.[6]

The idea that life, like God, may subject us to a severe ordeal in order to prove our mettle is well expressed in the following statement: **He took all that life could throw at him, and endured**. The believer may even be seen as fighting back, like Jacob who wrestled all night with God at the brook Jabbok.[7] Henry David Thoreau tackled life in the same way at Walden, and we now quite often hear of **wrestling with life** and of **taking life by the throat**.

Continuity between the old religion and the new may also extend to institutions. Not long ago – as older readers will recall – Catholic-minded Christians used to have a 'spiritual director', often an experienced older priest, who guided the development of their spiritual life. Today the director has been replaced by the **life coach**, who is an all-round guru, a combination of personal trainer, priest, therapist, and manager.

One more new discovery needs to be recalled here, because it enriches the whole argument and is a striking example of early life-talk. It is John Ruskin's Essay IV, 'Ad Valorem', in *Unto This Last* (1862), written soon after the publication of Darwin's *Origin of Species* when Ruskin was struggling to reformulate his personal creed. He is a critic of emergent modern capitalism and what it is doing to the human spirit. He wants to be able to appeal to something higher than economics and the laws of the market, but he has just lost his faith, and what he appeals to has to be immanent. So he comes up with the formula that **value is what avails for life** – a formula that some will see as proto-Nietzschean.

Here Ruskin joins hands with Wordsworth and Lawrence. He wants to invoke and to ground his values in something greater, older, and more general than contemporary political and economic theories and relations. He finds what he is looking for in the idea of **life**. And perhaps within a very few decades environmental problems will force us to make the same move, as we look for something higher than the world economy, or the strength of the dollar, to appeal to.

These few examples from the new material that has come my way recently are enough to remind us that in ordinary speech the word 'life' has undergone remarkable changes in the past forty-five years. Some nineteenth-century figures prepared the way, but it has all come home to ordinary people – and in ordinary speech – only since the rather sudden collapse of traditional Western Christianity that began in Europe during the 1960s. A great deal of religious imagery, thought, and feeling has shifted from God to **life;** indeed the bulk of the population are currently rethinking their religion. It is changing over from God-centred to life-centred. One is particularly struck by the persistence of certain vivid metaphors, and by the continuing strength of the impulse to personify life – even as a kind of beloved antagonist. Does this indicate that the 'life religion' of the future is going to make the same philosophical mistakes as the 'god religion' of the past?

Probably not. The most vivid idioms (**life's a bitch, wrestling with life, taking life by the throat, life is deaf, we don't control life** and so on) are noticeably ironical. We use them a little mockingly, with the same good humour as we use the residually theistic **someone up there is trying to tell you something** when a friend has a piece of bad luck, or **someone up there is keeping an eye on you** if someone has a narrow escape. Nowadays Westerners are as much aware as Orientals that religion is full of popular myths and convenient personifications, and the new religion of life is not likely to become dogmatic in the way that theism did. It has no creed, no priesthood, and indeed no organization into a distinct sacred society; it can therefore hope to retain its suppleness and linguistic liveliness. That is a good thing.

Life Force

Luigi Galvani (1737-1798) was Professor of Anatomy at the University of Bologna. In 1791 he published a curious new observation: a prepared frog's leg contracted sharply on being touched by a piece of charged metal. Galvani recognized that the muscular movement was being brought about by electricity, but was very unclear about how the electricity itself was being generated (and got himself into a controversy with Volta about that point). As it turned out, Galvani became famous anyway, because he established in the language an association that has remained with us, between 'galvanism', electricity, life, and a sharp jolt or kick. To galvanize somebody means to jolt him into life, the implication being that electricity itself is the life force.

Galvani thus gave new impetus to the old tradition that associates life with movement and has always tended to see the life principle in us as (metaphorically at least) a natural force. Life is like heat or fire in such idioms as **a spark of life** and **a flicker of life**, and it is like wind in idioms such as **the breath of life** and **the kiss of life**. Electricity, which before the twentieth century seemed to be such a mysterious, crackling and almost supernatural force, fitted very readily into that tradition. But because electricity seemed to be on the borderline between the natural and the supernatural, the material and the spiritual, it got built into some very questionable myths.

The most important example of this is Mary Wollstonecraft Shelley's *Frankenstein* (1818). In the version of the myth that became familiar through the cinema, Frankenstein is a renegade medical student, and almost from the beginning a damned soul who is trying to 'play God'. In his laboratory he creates a quasi-human monster, and brings it to life by throwing a great switch and sending a sharp jolt of electricity through it. The monster wakes to become its maker's doom.

This myth, which has reached us all, has an interesting mixture of ancient and modern motifs. Symbolically it suggests that life, which truly belongs to God, is an element properly belonging in the upper regions of the cosmos – above the spheres of air and fire, where the lightning comes from. Could it be the quintessence? In the nineteenth century some people even equated electricity with spirit. But if electricity is indeed some kind of natural force or energy, men of science may perhaps wish to study it and learn to control it. Or is it supernatural – and do they thereby risk supernatural retribution?

It's all hokum, but it is still with us. The doubt about whether life is a supernatural or a natural force lingered amongst some respectable scientists until the 1960s, when the rise of phrases like *molecular biology* shows that people have at last become persuaded that biology, that is, life, is in principle thoroughly reducible to chemistry. Even then, phrases like **life is sacred** and **all life belongs to God** persist, and medical science still runs into public criticism when it seems to be playing with the origin and the end of life and thereby to be trespassing upon God's territory. In addition, beyond respectable science – for example, in alternative medicine and the New Religious Movements – there is still much portentous talk of 'spiritual' *forces* and *energies,* to say nothing of **the life force** itself, which has been established in the language now for over a century.

As I say, it's all hokum, but it is still with us. The myth of the presumptuous, doomed scientist who tries to wield over life and death a power that properly belongs to God alone, and who is severely punished for it – this myth was subsequently established in the science fiction tradition by H.G. Wells's Dr Moreau, and in the ghost story and horror tradition by M.R. James. In Britain in recent years it has prompted ugly outbursts of public hostility to hospital pathologists, and to 'vivisectionists' (that is, physiologists). We should beware of anything that may encourage the mad scientist myth to flare up again.

In the last sentence of *The Origin of Species*, Darwin himself gave some encouragement to vitalism, by suggesting a supernatural cause for the very first appearance of life on earth. Commending his theory to sceptics in language chosen with a view to calming their fears, he says that

> There is grandeur in this view of life, with its several powers, having been originally breathed by the Creator into a few forms or one...[1]

This passage is compatible with what some commentators call 'nomothetic creation',[2] the idea that the first creation of life on earth was 'special' and supernatural, but thereafter life has been transmitted by purely natural means from one species to another, and from each generation to the next. A believer might say that God continues to create and give life, but does it through laws. But it would have been better for Darwin not to have introduced the contrast between supernaturalism and naturalism into his text at all.

Normally, Darwin's own instincts were correctly uniformitarian, and in any case the general rules of intellectual virtue in these matters are simple: one should never allow supernaturalism to get a firm foothold anywhere. Today, natural science still looks for one-level continuity in its account of nature, and philosophy insists that language is a continuum, and that the human life world is a continuum.

In the present book, whenever we speak of life we are always talking in the first instance about human social and historical existence, mediated by a continuous buzz of linguistic exchange, and set in the human life-world. We have every reason to enjoy tracing the immensely rich and varied metaphors that surround the idea of life. But we do not want to have anything to do with the reifying of biological life as a natural or supernatural 'force'. We should avoid anything that might help to revive ugly old myths about forbidden knowledge and mad scientists.

Loving Life

In a recent essay, *On Religion*, John D. Caputo asks the question 'What is it that we love when we love God?'[1] Good question. One line of reply might be to point out that God is defined as pure, absolute Love itself, so that to love God is simply to be in love with Love – the idea of love, being in love, and filled with love. Perhaps the best way of explaining what it is to love God, then, is to say that someone who loves God lives a life that is filled with love and transfigured by love. But love is not itself a single distinct thing, nor is there one single distinct thing that is loved. One who loves God lives in love objectlessly, since a religious attitude or disposition is not focused on one particular thing, but is universal or 'open'.

Today we do not hear much talk of loving God; in fact, people use the phrase so seldom that we feel that it calls for explanation. But the phrase **loving life** has become very common, and nobody questions it. So let us see if we can explain loving life in a way parallel to our explanation of loving God.

You ask, 'What is it that we love when we love life?' Good question. The best line of reply points out that life is not a substance, not a single, distinct thing that is singled out and fixed upon as a love object. Life is just the ongoing process of living: as people say, **Life is for living**. There are many living things, and many living persons, each of which has **a life to live**. Their **common life** involves continual multiple processes of exchange with each other and with their environment. Through these processes of exchange they build up around themselves a rich and complex **life world**.

Thus life is not a thing: it is **the business of living**, of plunging into the multiple processes of exchange – chemical, biological, economic, symbolic – through which the human cultural world, the life world, is generated, maintained and developed. And if we see then that life is not a thing, but simply the business of living, then to love life is to love living. One who loves life has a strong **appetite for life**: she is always, as the new phrase goes, **up for it**, keen to join in, ready for anything. One who loves life loves the business of living, because she relishes – I mean she actively enjoys and looks forward to – new experiences and the various forms of exchange (such as food, sex, talk and so forth) that living involves. Through these many exchanges both we and our world are being changed all the time, and anyone who loves life has to be a person who is happy to change. She finds the whole business of socializing, change, and exchange *intoxicating*. Some people enjoy life so much and so obviously that they inspire others with the same enjoyment. Of such a person one may say that **she is the life and soul of the party**.

One may bring out the difference between a person who loves life and a person who is inclined to withdraw from life by saying that the latter kind of person typically tries to **keep himself to himself**. He fears that the business of living will involve leakage, contamination, and loss of identity, and he therefore prefers to keep apart; whereas the life loving type of person paradoxically seeks personal fulfillment through self-giving and exchange, and makes no effort to preserve the self unchanged.

No, life is not a single distinct thing, and someone who loves life is not a person who has fixed upon just one single love-object, but one who delights in the daily business of living. As Spinoza was once called 'a god-intoxicated man', so one who loves life may be called life-intoxicated. Such a person revels in transience. As people say in this connection: **it gives me a buzz, it makes me feel more alive, it turns me on**. Having said earlier that one who loves God lives in objectless love we may now add that one who loves life loves the business of living so much as to get from it **a permanent high**. She has an enhanced vitality, or *Lebensgefühl*.

At the opposite extreme, the person who shrinks from life, perhaps because her morale or her vitality are low, or perhaps because she feels she's **out of it**, is liable to slip into social isolation and a kind of fetishism of routine – a *rut*, as people say. People tend to get this way if they live in villages, which appropriately enough are commonly described as 'sleepy'. Life there is very quiet. Little happens; people do not *want* anything to happen.

From this brief discussion I conclude that the logic of loving life is very similar to the logic of loving God. At least, I have interpreted both of them non-realistically. But loving life usually promotes a somewhat different ethical stance than does loving God. The person who loves life makes a point of not acknowledging any distinction between the religious and secular realms. She simply finds spiritual value and fulfillment in commitment to ordinary social life. She likes the ordinary physical business of living; she likes mingling and mixing, joining in and taking on. (I have made this character female because of course it is Woman who is most obviously changed by the exchanges in which she gets involved.) By contrast, the person who loves God tends to make a distinction between religious and secular concerns and, at least from time to time, probably turns away from the human world to attend specifically to God. This rather traditional believer is apt to find the human world tiring and distracting. Attention to God 'recollects', calms, and refreshes him.

However, it is nowadays possible to find a few modernists amongst the believers. These are people whose love for God finds expression only through love for life, and in their case there isn't any great difference between 'God' and 'life' as religious concerns – a point we need to emphasize in order to help people make the transition from the god-centred religion of the past to the secular and life-centred religion of today.

The Love of His Life

Most of the time we seem able to draw a clear distinction between two sorts of love, fixated love and 'open' love.

Fixated love is love that is locked on to a single finite object that it has chosen and is securely committed to. It is love that has been *aroused by* an object, and that *has fixed upon* the object. Human sexual love, and most other human loves, are normally of this kind. Open love, by contrast, is an objectless, non-fixated universal disposition. One is *in* it, filled with it, and one feels it towards all the world, **for no particular reason**, as people say, just as one may also feel universal, objectless, no-particular-reason joy or happiness. **The love of God** is perhaps the chief example of open love. God is said to be infinite, and therefore is not some kind of object 'out there' upon which love can fasten or fixate. Nothing that is objectively existent can be infinite. So the love of God is not love for any object, but is open, universal and non-selective. It shapes one's whole being, and all one's attitudes: it fills one's whole life.

At this point in the argument we can briefly comment on the question of 'atheism'. Atheism is perfectly correct in that indeed there is not an actual being out there to be named or referred to as God. But once we have understood that there is no being out there, we can begin to give an accurate account of what it is to love God. Only *via* atheism can we reach a correct understanding of theistic spirituality.

Setting aside, for our present purposes, any further discussion of that point, I ask you to grant me the broad distinction between *fixated* love (love for a finite object) and *open*, objectless, 'sacred' love. Open love, the love of God, is boundless or infinite: it has no object; but when one is *in* it, it changes one's whole life. It is worth remarking that both 'Love' and 'Life' are popular non-realist names of God, much used in hymnody.

Clear enough. But there are cases where ordinary human fixated love grows so intense that it spills over and begins to appropriate religious language and acquire a religious character. These cases are very interesting. The best mark of them is the tendency to conjoin the word *love* with the word *life*, as in the phrase **the love of his life**. In *Wuthering Heights*, Heathcliff speaks of Catherine Earnshaw both as his *life* and as his *soul*. When she dies, he cries out: 'I *cannot* live without my life! I *cannot* live without my soul!'[1] In such words human love takes on a religious quality.

In the West, human love has borrowed the vocabulary of religion since the Middle Ages. Phrases like **he worships her** have become clichés, and we no longer examine them closely. But perhaps we should, and I take as an example one that I have noted very recently: **My dove, my love, my life! My dove** is comparable with my bird, or pet or doll: the beloved is a cherishable finite object. **My love** speaks of the beloved as being so close as to be like a part of oneself, or as being scarcely distinguishable from the love that loves her, or the eye that sees her: **the apple of my eye, the light of my eyes**. The third phrase, **my life**, speaks of the beloved as almost indwelling the speaker and as irradiating his entire life. Here the word **life** indicates that although the beloved is still a finite object, love for her has expanded to fill the lover's life, and affect all his attitudes. It has become something that is with him all the time, wherever he goes. It animates his whole existence. In short, it has become religious.

Something similar is happening in the case where we speak of a great love as **the love of his life**. We are a little cautious about using this phrase, considering it to be justified only if the person in question has proved willing to sacrifice or at least change the direction of his whole life for his love's sake, or if the two have been devoted lovers for more than half of their lives. In short, a great love, the love of one's life, has the sort of unrivalled primacy in one's life as a whole that God might otherwise have. It is also in its own way 'monotheistic', for it has never been suggested that there could possibly be more than one great love in

anyone's life, either simultaneously or serially. A great love is by defini-
tion one that has become the central and dominant concern of a person's life and as such it is of course unique.

It now needs to be asked whether a great love, by appearing to put a
finite fellow creature in the place of God in one's life, involves heresy or
– worse – idolatry. A Muslim would surely find it so, because in Islam
the divine and the human, God and man, infinite and finite, remain
strictly distinct. Islam is never humanistic. It never wants to transfer
divine attributes to a human being, nor to ascribe ordinary human qual-
ities to God. But Latin Christianity, at least since the rise of *amour cour-
tois* in medieval France, seems to have been much more indulgent – no
doubt because the faith had always presented believers not only with
the invisible God, but also with a range of permitted finite *human* objects
of devotion and veneration: the human Jesus, Mary and so on. If a nun
could take Jesus as her Bridegroom, and if a priest could be romantically
devoted to Mary, why should not human lovers inject religious vocabulary into their relations with their ladies? In fact, the Christian tradition
had always allowed a certain two-way mingling of the vocabularies of
sexual and divine love. It was canonized in the long tradition of interpreting a collection of secular love songs in the Bible, the *Song of Songs*,
as a mystical allegory. Earlier still, even the relation between Israel and
her Lord Yahweh had been described in erotic language in the Hebrew
Bible. Evidently the Judaeo-Christian tradition has always accepted the
possibility that human love might expand to fill someone's life and so
take on universal, religious significance.

Why is it, though, that if ordinary human love is to swell and
become divine, it must do so by becoming closely associated with the
word **life**, rather than with other totalizing words such as 'it,' 'it all,' and
'things'?

On inspection of the relevant idioms, it very soon turns out to be
true that these other totalizing words (**it, it all** and **things**), together with
other and older words such as **fate, destiny** and **chance**, do attract a
good deal of displaced god-talk nowadays. We use all these words in
order to refer in a vague and non-committal way to 'the nature of things',
or to the large but little understood background against which our life is
set. Often our uses are rather complaining: **I find it all a bit too much**,
we say, or **Things are getting me down**. On the whole, *it* and *things* are
cool and unfriendly: language very rarely seems to find **it all** benevolent
and loving towards us. The great advantage of the word **life** stems from
the fact that it is anchored in the world of persons, their feelings and

their values, and it reaches out to encompass everything. The word **life** links the personal with the cosmic. Its huge range of use helps us to situate ourselves in the world, and to project our own point of view and values over everything. It is perhaps by this route that **life** has become our most important totalizing word, which in recent years has been replacing God.

Life Doesn't Stop

People have always liked the idea that there may be gaps in the world, and it crops up in many different forms in religious myth, in children's literature, and in science fiction. If we had some way of detecting and making use of gaps in space and time, we might be able to vanish suddenly from where we are and then step back into this world at some quite different point. It might be that somewhere on earth there is a cave through which, like Dante, one can descend to the underworld.[1] Or by climbing a sacred Mountain we might reach the Heavenly world, as Moses and Aaron, Nadab and Abihu and the rest of their delegation did when they ascended Sinai,[2] and saw God enthroned with his feet planted on the upper surface of the blue vault of the sky.

In children's literature the parallel universe to which the author and his reader long to return is fairyland, the world of the imagination, the world of early childhood or perhaps a looking-glass world. Often it is reached simply by falling asleep, or by opening a small and inconspicuous door that will turn out to be very hard to find again.

Another sort of gap in the world opens up when the ordinary limits of people's powers are suspended for a while. A woman becomes a sibyl or a prophetess; a man becomes a superhero or a miracle-worker; someone discovers a short cut to knowledge of the future, or the fulfillment of wishes. Through dreams such as these, the powerless are able for a while to forget their powerlessness.

Such stories of gaps in the world are as diverse as they are seductive, but their magical fascination is no indicator of their plausibility, for we recognize that this is never how things are in fact. The human life world is continuous and flowing, and we never come to any gaps in it. Indeed, the very reason why we speak of life as flowing and of time as a river is that, unlike a wall, which *can* have a gap in it, a river cannot. A liquid flows continuously, with no gaps. And so it is with the life world: like the visual field, it is always continuous. We never actually *see* a hole in the visual field, nor do we ever come to its edge when we turn our heads. Just as the sense of sight always gives us a complete and endless world, so the life world is always complete and endless, and language is always complete and endless. Every point in space is *there*, just where it should be; and every point in time duly comes up and then recedes, just as expected. There are no gaps. That is the true meaning of the ancient neoplatonic idea that the world is a *plenum*: language structures the world in such a way as to lay out as wide and complete a field of possibilities as may be. There is a certain sort of logical completeness that every natural language has, and that every natural language ascribes to the world.

There are no gaps. The life world is always complete and continuous, and it all moves together. It does not stop. Nowhere does time stand still, nowhere can you get off, rest awhile, and then get on again at your leisure. On the contrary, if you become **tired of life** and lazy, and allow yourself to drop out for a while, you will very soon be heard complaining, '**I feel that life has passed me by**'. *You* may stop, and in death you certainly do so; but **life does not stop**. It goes on.

Hobbes and Nietzsche offer us the best reminders that life is *unresting*, that it actually consists in 'a perpetual and restless desire of power after power, that ceaseth only in death'[3] or a continual casting about for whatever will refresh and enhance its own appetite for itself. And to this Malthus and Darwin have added the 'struggle for existence', an important idea, and one well worth dwelling on for a moment. There are various strands in it.

First, zoologists have long recognized the importance of what they call 'appetitive behaviour', which is the living animal's busy ferreting about, seeking, exploring, casting around – behaviour by which it continuously explores its environment, looks out for food or a mate, and finds the best places to shelter and rest in. Appetitive behaviour is found in animals of all kinds from protozoa to primates, and its advantageousness is obvious. In order to optimize its chances of survival, an animal needs to explore its environment thoroughly and continuously, discovering and learning which bits of the environment are rewarding and which dangerous.

That is one sense in which life cannot afford to stop and idle. A second is this: it is a general principle in physiology that a stimulus repeated without change provokes less and less response. The animal becomes numbed. For its senses to remain fresh and alert, and itself keyed-up, an animal needs to seek and to enjoy novel stimuli. Amongst humans these two principles are most familiarly illustrated in the fields of sex and food, fashion and catering. We don't just want the same every day, forever; on the contrary, to keep ourselves 'turned on' we need continual slight change – and that includes not just changes in fashion, or in design, or in cooking, for there is also a continual quest in popular language for clever and appealing new descriptive *words* and *phrases*. This perpetual restless movement of public taste is perhaps the principal motor of cultural change.

The third strand in the doctrine that life doesn't and cannot stop was first described really well (so far as I know) by Meister Eckhart: it is the somewhat puzzling and fascinating fact that life lives by and for its own ceaseless, upwelling joy in itself. Life is impelled by **the joy of life**, the **rage for life**. This idea is the equivalent in life theology of the doctrine of God's 'aseity' in traditional theology. God is 'from himself', God is himself the ground of his own existence; in no way does God need to be proved or validated or guided by anything external to himself. Eckhart, when he speaks of life as its own ground, intrinsically desirable, and unanswerably affirming itself, seems to assimilate life to God: 'God's being is my life'.[4]

Such are the three principal strands in the idea that life doesn't stop: endlessly and restlessly, life pours itself out, always seeking more of itself, actively relishing novelty, and rejoicing in its own self-enhancement and self-propagation. One sees here an area in which one day somebody will elaborate a systematic theology of life. But I am certainly not going to do *that*, for if it were successful it would surely get turned into a dogma and would be used to bully people.

Chapter 27

The Doctor Pronounced Life Extinct

Life does not stop. In the cultural realm this is a refutation of the traditionalist claim that what we have received from the past is sacred and immutable. Change happens, and it cannot be stopped. Why? Because cultural life simply consists in an unceasing process of symbolic exchange, through which all meanings and values, myths and institutions gradually shift in response to changes in the climate of opinion and in public taste. Whether we like it or not, the life world simply *is* rest-less and everchanging – as all who live in a developed consumer society are intensely aware.

But doesn't life stop in death? The obvious response to this is to point out that although the individual **lifespan** is finite, life itself goes on. The individual drops out of it, but the conversation of society in general continues indefinitely. It existed before the individual and it will continue after him. There is a biological version of this point in the late nineteenth-century doctrine taught by August Weismann (1834-1914) to the effect that our reproductive tissue, the 'germ-plasm', is immortal.[1] The individual organism is only a temporary vehicle that carries the germ-plasm for a generation and then passes it on. Today many people say something similar about the DNA: the individual may die, but the DNA goes on, continuously shaking itself into fresh configurations, and adapting itself to new conditions. So we stop, indeed – but life goes on.

These rather familiar arguments create a somewhat uncomfortable dissonance with which everyone is familiar today. The individual's span of life is relatively brief, and the contribution he or she can hope to make is miniscule by comparison with the vastness of the ongoing life world's public conversation – especially in the age of globalization, and in the English language as it is today.

Remember: thinking is only internalized speaking. Its coinage consists only of words and other signs – public objects, whose current meanings (or ways of moving) are determined out there in the public realm and simply presented to us. We can think only in the currently available vocabulary, and this means that the current state of the culture limits the range of what we can think much more strictly than at first appears. So powerful, indeed, are the mass media in contemporary society that it is not easy for anyone to be a free thinker: one's best chance of getting any leverage against the vast public consensus is by pointing out and making the most of tensions and contradictions within it.

The problem then, is that although people are freer, richer, and better educated than they have ever been, we are not doing as well as we should be; for the public communications media are overwhelmingly larger and more powerful than the single individual, and they tend to be dominated by a limited number of great corporations. The effect is that they tend to make our life rather 'samey', as people say. In a genial but overwhelming way, they severely limit thought. It is not surprising that so many people are worried about death, finitude and the significance of the individual. Nor is it at all surprising that the professions which chiefly control our entrance into life and our exit from it – I mean, the medical and paramedical professions – have become so important, and so highly pressured.

The doctor pronounced life extinct: you recognise the phrase, and you hazard a guess that it comes from a mid-nineteenth-century novel, perhaps by Wilkie Collins or Sheridan Le Fanu. The phrase comes from a time when the most important professional person who attends a deathbed has become the medical man. He has risen to replace his old rival the priest, who is now in decline. It is his task formally to declare or pronounce that death has taken place, and to write a death certificate on which he states his opinion as to the cause of death. Being a man of science, he regards life as a natural phenomenon, whose typical signs are bodily warmth and a variety of bodily motions. When all the motions have ceased, and the body is cooling, life can be judged extinct. The metaphor of extinction (= extinguishment, or quenching) is drawn chiefly from fires, volcanoes and candle-flames. In the texts of both Plato and the Buddha, death is compared with the extinguishment of a candle, or it is simply presumed that the individual life ceases when somebody dies.[2] Thus the doctor's takeover at the deathbed implies the end of serious belief in life after death. Society's prime concern is no longer to ensure that the dying person makes a good transition to her place in the next world: all we want to know is that the death has indeed occurred, and from natural causes, so that — to return to the Victorian novel — we can get on with reading the will and distributing the property.

If that is the change that has taken place, then we can see why the priest has declined so greatly in importance, and the doctor has risen correspondingly. We see why the doctor has become such a powerful and respected figure, and also why he attracts some resentment. He is the bringer of bad news, at least about the long-term importance of the individual. But the best response to the realization that there is no life after death is *not* to blame the messenger who brings the bad news, *nor* to cast about desperately for some consolation and substitute, but to take to heart the classic Epicurean teaching that 'death is nothing to us'. There is nothing there, and certainly nothing that one can usefully spend time preparing oneself for. The rational response is to forget about death, and simply to concentrate our attention upon life now. Instead of dreaming about a heaven beyond the grave, we should seek to 'eternalize' our life in the here and now. When we have learnt to find eternal happiness in the present moment, we will no longer lament the loss of a rather questionable prospect of it hereafter.

Chapter 28

Private Life

In earlier chapters I have argued that although **life** is now our best totalizing word, a neatly systematic philosophy of life is not going to be possible. The word **life** includes everything, and excludes nothing. It includes the whole world of our experience, all our faiths and philosophies, and all our varied and conflicting world views and values. It embraces all the opposites of the human condition, the extremes of happiness and wretchedness, intelligibility and incomprehensibility, good and evil, familiarity and alienness, excess and emptiness. All this is too much to be arranged into a single rational system. The best we can do is to create a vision of what can be made of life, and live by that. And for my money, the best and noblest such vision is the comic vision – provided we recall that a certain disciplined generosity of spirit is going to be needed to carry it through.

We also argued earlier that just as life in general is so excessive in all directions that it cannot be systematized, so the life of the single human individual cannot be systematized in the old way either. From the Golden Age of Greece to the Enlightenment it was generally believed that there was a highest good, the supreme goal or *telos* of human life. This was 'man's chief end'. Philosophy called it 'the good', and religion called it 'the vision of God'. The good life for a human being was a fully examined, transparent life, with all the subultimate ends of action arranged in their proper rank order below the highest good, and with all of life's varied activities orchestrated by reason towards the eventual attainment of our chief end, final salvation. This fully rational and unified pattern of life was best exemplified by a monk whose whole life was directed towards the vision of God, and by the philosopher who was absorbed in contemplation of the good.

Such was the classic Western theory of **the good life**. But it represented an ideal **way of life** that could be followed only by a sequestered and highly privileged celibate elite. As during the later Middle Ages lay culture expanded and diversified, it naturally began to demand a version or versions of the good life that was accessible to lay people who lived in the world and had social responsibilities.

The solution that was found, both in Renaissance Italy and in proto-Protestant Northern Europe, involves making a rather sharp distinction between public and private **spheres of life** — between, for example, the rules you must apply in your public role as a magistrate, and the code you should live by as a private individual who is a sinner as much in need of salvation as anyone else. As public official, you had to follow a broadly Old Testament code, your guiding value being *justice*; but as private individual you should follow the gentler code of the Gospel, your guiding value being *mercy*.

For about 500 years we have followed some version of these ideas, which abandon the old dream of a fully unified life in favour of the modern doctrine that breaks our life up into distinct spheres that we need (and like) to keep separate. As we move from one sphere to another — which we do daily — we **put on a different hat**, as the saying goes: we assume different roles and somewhat different moral personalities. It is also notable that, as the years have passed, the original distinction between the official role and the private life has undergone a number of transformations.

As modern commercial-industrial society expanded, one such change arose from the separation of the house of business from the domestic residence. As early as the eighteenth century, some rich London bankers were moving their principal private residence out to such gentrified villages in Hertfordshire as Much Hadham. In the nineteenth century the railway made commuting a mass phenomenon, and people began to prefer the commuter's **double life**: townspeople by day, villagers by night. The time on the train has become a ritual transition between different worlds and different lives.

Another and very significant shift became apparent in the debates of the 1960s about public and private morality. The private sphere was originally understood in religious terms: it was the sphere of personal devotion, of religious experience, and of the individual's free pursuit of **the religious life**. But in the twentieth century the main emphasis came to be laid upon the pursuit of psychological emancipation through discovering, exploring, and freely expressing one's own sexuality.

The shift can be seen happening if we consider the original dates and life contexts of the following expressions, and their subsequent history:

> **the religious life**
> **the interior life**
> **the spiritual life**
> **private life**
> **love life**
> **sex life**
> **personal life**

Without getting sidetracked by fascinating historical detail, we can note here the very striking extent to which religion has been replaced by sex as the most popular source of the vocabulary we use to describe the quest for personal fulfillment. For many people today the pursuit of sexual fulfillment is something they guard as jealously and insist upon as determinedly as their ancestors used to insist upon and cherish their religious freedom.

I am not sure that I dare to say that these people are wrong. If we have only this life, and if it is indeed true that a state of settled sexual happiness with the right partner is for most people the chief of life's blessings, then perhaps the quest for sexual happiness fully deserves to play as prominent a part in modern people's lives as the quest for salvation used to play in the lives of people a few centuries ago. Why not?

Serious reservations are likely to be raised only when we ask why it is necessary to remove some activity into the sphere of private life, where it can be pursued out of sight and exempt from public scrutiny and criticism. When conducted within small and secluded sects, the pursuit of religious freedom and the exercise of the parents' right to determine the religious upbringing of their own children can involve serious abuse of power, cruelty, and irrationality; and the same is obviously true of the pursuit of sexual freedom within the sphere of 'personal' or 'private' life. With what motives are people brandishing words like *personal* or *private* and telling the public to back off?

A still more interesting and delicate question arises in connection with someone who takes a step further and lives **a double life**. If we are saying that we do not believe a systematic, metaphysically unified philosophy of life to be possible, and if we are also saying that we do not believe in a single metaphysical core self or rational soul, then why *shouldn't* a person live a double life? Many of us nowadays are like actors in being rather multiple, and in living rather different lives in different settings. Your own child behaves and speaks rather differently when with you at home, when at school, and when out late 'clubbing'. So imagine a male bigamist who successfully lives a double life. He is a good husband and father in two different families. He smoothly juggles two distinct lives and sets of relationships, and fulfils all his responsibilities in both settings. That is how he likes to live. Is his behaviour morally questionable? There *is* no one metaphysical self. Selfhood is theatrical, a matter of playing a role, and many people are in varying degrees multiple personalities who live more than one life. So is our ethical bigamist doing anything morally wrong, and if so, just what *makes* it wrong?

This is not an easy question to answer. It seems that only a very small minority of people nowadays can be expected to be old-style fully unified selves whose entire lives are integrated by one great overmastering goal. Indeed, that sort of single-issue, highly focussed person has become rather unattractive to most of us, anyway. But neither are we happy with some of the implications of the suggestion that we are all of us nowadays multiple personalities, living several lives and playing many distinct parts. We seem to be in an intermediate position. On the one hand, there is no one rational soul who is the morally accountable subject of our whole lives. Life nowadays is so excessive and chaotic that we are all of us a little pluralized. But we should beware of allowing the different sub-lives we live to become morally isolated from each other. We should think of ourselves as morally responsible for all the varied doings of the repertoire of characters that we play. Even if our lives aren't metaphysically uniform, we should try to think of ourselves as single moral subjects. I *think* so, but I am far from sure about the whole topic.

The Life in Your Man

According to Mae West, 'It's not **the man in your life** that counts, but the life in your man'. Her films are seldom shown nowadays and the famous sayings reach us mainly via oral tradition or from secondary sources, so that one suspects many of them of being apocryphal; but this one is at least *ben trovato*.[1] It makes the point that because of the huge influence of Schopenhauer and Freud, **the turn to life** in modern Western thought has also been a turn to the sex drive which at last recognizes its central role in the constitution of the person.[2] The word **libido** as we have come to use it comprehends, and more or less equates, what psychoanalysis called **the life instinct** and **the sex drive**. So **the life in your man** means his energy and stamina in bed. And there is no doubt that a great deal of life talk is surrounded by a cloud of sexual metaphors and allusions. Sex is life, and while you are sexually active you are still alive.

This fact helps to explain why we have so strong a tendency to personify life, to see it as a separate presence with whom we have to deal, and to experience sexuality as a comical, awkward other self within the self, sometimes a good deal too forward, at other times too retiring, and at all times oddly independent of our rational control. There is a strange mismatch between consciousness and sex – perhaps especially in males.

The main tradition of Western thought ever since Plato has tended to equate the 'real' core-self, the immortal soul that is oriented towards the heavenly world, with subjective consciousness. But in Schopenhauer there begins a new tradition that sees the sex drive as central to the constitution and maintenance of the self. This has the effect of partly displacing the conscious subject. Even during sleep, when subjective consciousness is in abeyance, the sex drive continues unaffected on its two-hour cycles, cranking up, generating and working through its fantasies and then calming down for a while. It is as if the sex drive goes on in its own way, not needing and *unaware of* consciousness. The sex drive and the conscious self are a comedy couple, funny man and straight man, two ill-assorted characters yoked very oddly together, sometimes quarrelling, sometimes independent, and sometimes getting along just fine. **O, isn't life a terrible thing, thank God?**[3]

If we acknowledge that the sex drive in us exhibits a dynamic of its own[4] largely independent of our rational control, and that it is in many ways like a greedy amoral child, then we begin to see why some forms of religion have striven so determinedly to master it. Osama bin Laden, the Islamic terrorist leader, sums up the position when he contrasts his people with those of the modern West. He boasts that his people love death as much as the Westerners love life. He is — or was, if he is no longer alive — *proud* to be a lover of death. He equates the love of life with moral decadence.

In what he says, bin Laden conjures up in stark and simplified form a clear contrast between two very different philosophies of the human being and human life. It is worth setting them out briefly: I'll call them the Old Model and the New Model.

The Old Model

Traditional religious believers are lovers of death. For them the core self is the subjectively conscious self, the immortal soul, which is distinct from the body and is oriented towards the hope of final salvation in the world to come after death. Life should be spent in purifying the soul in preparation for death. Because of its intellectual and social subversiveness, the sex drive needs to be strictly regulated in accordance with the revealed will of God. It must not be permitted to distract the soul from its pursuit of its proper goals.

The New Model

Modern Westerners, by contrast, are lovers of life and of the pleasures of this world. For them the core self is libido itself, which continually pours itself out in symbolic representation. Cultural life is a libido-driven dance of signs: the richer and more varied, the better. Muslim and other puritans complain that in the West sex is used to sell every-thing, but they shouldn't be surprised, for sex – understood in a broad sense, as libido – *powers* everything. As for consciousness, it simply *floats* upon the dance of signs. So modern Westerners love life, love art, and love free, authentic self-expression. We have largely broken away from the old death-oriented kind of religion which saw life as a struggle for purity, and as a final battle between good and evil. For us, joy in life has become the chief end of life: hence all the dozens of idioms of **welling up, bubbling, glowing, sparkling, shining, zest** and **appetite** in which we express the exhilaration of life. *Jouissance* is spirit is **high spirits.**

The old model is approximately rationalist and platonic. It sees life as a journey, and the conscious self as being much concerned with self-mastery, self-purification and keeping one's eyes steadfastly fixed upon life's final destination. By contrast, the new model is post-darwinian and very short-termist. It sees our life much more in terms of theatre and dance, and presupposes that in the past we were too gloomily preoccu-pied with objective knowledge and conscious *control* – both of ourselves and of the environment.

I like this stark contrast between the old model and the new model. It helps one to see the issues really clearly, and forces a clear choice. I am increasingly a purely new-model person. I like the metaphysical nihilism of the new model, because for me universal emptiness is spiri-tual clarity and purity. I like the sparkling beauty and 'brightness' of the new-model vision of the world. I like the new-model idea of the unity of religion and the sex drive: that is, I like the way libido flowing through us gives colour to the world, makes it dazzlingly beautiful, and turns into religious joy. That's redemption, new style.

My critics hate the way I set up stark oppositions and demand a choice. It's not as simple as that, they splutter indignantly. And they may well wish to point to the Baroque Catholicism that emerged in and after the Council of Trent, for it was profoundly this-worldly and humanistic. In the Rococo it even became new-model, while yet wholly and uninhibitedly Catholic. Surely Baroque Catholicism achieved a syn-thesis of my opposites, and therefore shows that I am wrong to set them up as irreconcilable alternatives between which one must choose.

No, I do not retract at all. It is true that the Baroque style tries to reconcile Catholicism and Humanism, death and life, the next world and this life, mystical union and unabashed sex; but it was all achieved under the aegis of an overwhelming affirmation of pure power. Power comes first, power always controls truth, power keeps all the binary pairs firmly distinct and, in fact, *un*reconciled. The Baroque was violently repressive, and its legacy is the sadly damaged religious psychology about which the shocked laity have been learning in recent years. In fact, neither the most liberal Protestantism nor the most humanistic Catholicism gets anywhere near the reform of religion that is required today. (And if I permit myself any qualification to that, it will be in favour of only the dreamiest and dizziest late Rococo.)

Chapter 30

The Body of Life

It is a very odd choice of metaphor, but we quite often find the whole of life – i.e., the whole life world – being compared with a living body and seen as having its own pulsating rhythm, its own tempi. I think the point of it is that our own individual subjectivity is not quite as free-standing or as important as it likes to think. It is only an epiphenomenon; it floats upon and is shaped by life rhythms, both individual and social, that ebb and flow largely independently of it and of which it knows little.

Here's a first illustration of the point. Some time ago I waited by a deathbed in company with a senior doctor, who murmured that the dying person had come to the stage where all the body's various systems, functions and rhythms were beginning to shut down one after another. We watched this happening. It was rather eerily methodical – as if life itself was moving quietly around inside, throwing switches, turning things off, putting up the shutters, and preparing shortly to vacate the premises. The process was lengthy: it took several hours, and the dying person had been unconscious for some time already. So I was made aware of how many life systems and rhythms there are inside us that normally go about their business unremarked. We depend upon them for the maintenance of our subjective life, but most of the time we are unconscious of them and they cheerfully disregard us.

Another example is the circadian rhythms. In 1992 I had a craniotomy which seems to have disturbed them, so that the complicated machinery that comes into operation at bedtime, winding us down and getting us ready for a good night's sleep, was damaged. This made *me* aware of something you may not have noticed – that every night's sleep is a kind of mini-hibernation for which our physiology makes a number of preparations.

In these two cases I became aware of life's mysterious goings-on within the body because I saw the consequences of their being disrupted. In a third case, that of the sex-drive, which was mentioned in the last chapter, life again surges along, following its own rhythm – but in this case the drive is so strong that it regularly (and perhaps *normally*) obtrudes upon our awareness. It makes our nerves tingle, heightens our sensibility and fills with ideas the heads of artists. Every 90 or 120 minutes during sleep it seems to prompt a period of rapid-eye-movement sleep, dreaming, and erotic excitation. In a word, it seems that libido is stronger than the other life rhythms, so strong that it enhances all our sense experience and colours the way language moves in our brains. It profoundly influences consciousness all the time, and no doubt we are all aware of it. It shows up in ordinary language as **the feeling of being alive,** *Lebensgefühl,* **joie de vivre, the joys of life,** and so on. It gives **spice** or **zest** to an existence which would be very grey without it.

These considerations have already led us to think that traditional Western ideas of self-mastery were mistaken. It was asserted that in each human being reason should govern the passions and control the body, as a charioteer controls his horses and steers his chariot. And as these ideas have reached us after Descartes, we have tended to go further, and to suppose that the 'I', the conscious individual subject, can be and should be something like the absolute monarch of 'my body' and 'my life'.

These ideas are clearly wrong. A human being is not a sovereign, rational spirit in a house of clay, but a biological organism. Consciousness, I have been suggesting, is an epiphenomenon of 'life': in us life pours out in symbolic expression as a stream of language, and when the stream of symbols turns back upon itself and refers to itself, it generates consciousness. Thus conscious rational thought is not something primary and foundational in the constitution of the world, but a secondary latecomer. David Hume makes the point in one of his best-known lines:

> We speak not strictly and philosophically when we talk
> of the combat of passion and of reason. Reason is, and ought

only to be the slave of the passions, and can never pretend to
any other office than to serve and obey them.[1]

Opposing Augustan rationalism, writers like Hume and the young
Wordsworth urge us to recognize that 'Nature', or the passions, or 'the
heart', comes first. Today, our way of making the same point is to say
that subjective consciousness and rational control have been ranked too
high. *Life* comes first. We need to start thinking more biologically.

So far in this section we have talked about life mainly in the biological sense, and mainly at the level of the individual. We have now to turn
to the suggestion that at the social and cultural level too, 'life' has its
own seemingly autonomous pace, rhythms and tempi. Here we are talking about something that began to emerge during the eighteenth century, between Vico and Hegel, as ideas about historical change and about
culture gradually developed. The English language was slow to pick up
on the new thinking, but we did at least appreciate that the world was
becoming better informed and more democratic, and that in a democra-
tized society there is something called 'public opinion' that one should
take note of. In the early nineteenth century writers like William Hazlitt
(1825) and R.H. Horne introduced into English phrases such as **the spirit
of the age** and **the climate of opinion**. The idea that each historical
period has its own distinctive style of thinking, set of assumptions and so
on (just as it has its own styles in women's clothing, furniture and all
other consumer products) has now become a cliché. People speak confi-
dently – perhaps dismissively – about **the Fifties, the Sixties** and **the
Eighties**, as if a new world view, a new ethic, and a new style of decora-
tion were born with each new decade. Nowadays indeed, as soon as each
new decade begins, its debut is scrutinized by journalists competing to
define its principal characteristics and an incessant media demand arises
for a new generation of young artists to lionize, with the unhappy result
that large numbers of mature artists who emerged in earlier decades find
themselves often permanently and quite unfairly neglected and out of
fashion.

Such excesses aside, our language makes it evident that we recognize
that deep cultural change is going on all the time, and that it goes on in
every area of the culture. It affects fashions in clothing and in taste, but it
also affects moral values, world view, religious attitudes, and philosophy.
Hegel thought he could describe an immanent logic in the way such
changes go; but today we are sure to be much more cautious than he was.
Deep change happens. We can see that it is very kind to those authors
and ideas that it brings back into fashion, and very unkind to others,

highly regarded only yesterday, whom it suddenly thrusts aside. But we do not know the logic of these strange shifts. Sometimes we express the hope that from the abrupt ups and downs of fashion a fairer valuation of each artist and writer will eventually emerge, but nothing guarantees it. Why is the novelist Angus Wilson so forgotten? Will he ever be reinstated? We have no idea.

How far do considerations such as these justify the comparison of the whole world of cultural life with a living body that has laws, rhythms and tempi of its own? The suggestion we often hear goes something like this: the individual person is apt to imagine that his own body is transparent to him and will do whatever he requires of it. But the conscious subject is not as sovereign as it thinks it is, and we all of us should pay more heed to the rhythms of life in our own bodies, to 'the heart' and 'the passions'. Such current English phrases as **emotional intelligence** remind us of these points.

Similarly, the argument continues, in the great public conversation of society much more is going on than many people recognize. The shallowness of our understanding of our own culture is indicated by the use of phrases such as **talking heads** and **the chattering classes**. The suggestion is that 'the intellectuals' are often unsatisfactory spokesmen for the whole life of the culture, very much as subjective consciousness, the 'I', is an unsatisfactory spokesman for the whole life of the person. As the 'I' needs to attend more carefully to the life of the body and the passions, so intellectuals need to be more aware of the semi-autonomous life of the culture as a whole, and the deep shifts and adjustments that it is currently struggling to make.

I think that's correct. A very long tradition in mythology and in political thought compares the state with a body, the body politic. In addition, a two-centuries-old tradition going back to German writers such as Schiller and von Humboldt speaks of language as 'an activity' and as 'living', and of culture as a continuous process of symbolic exchange. So it seems natural enough to speak of goings-on in the cultural realm as **cultural life**. And if we are inquiring about what deep cultural change is and why it happens, we may guess that it follows some sort of *bio-logic* which at present is unknown to us.

With even greater confidence I will assert that in retrospect we can often tell a *story* about cultural change, but we cannot produce a scientific *theory* of it.

Chapter 31

All Life Is Six to Five against

> In fact', Sam the Gonoph says, 'I long ago came to the conclusion that all life is six to five against.'
> Damon Runyon, *More Than Somewhat*, 'A Nice Price'

Why does Sam the Gonoph think that on the whole and in the long run life always turns out to be against us? Why indeed is everyone in the end a loser? Because we are constitutionally prone to expect of life a more consistent moral policy towards us than it ever has.

The problem arises because our brains work by scanning the environment in search of significant events, regular patterns and, indeed, *narrative* patterns. We want to be able to read the chain of life events as a meaningful narrative – and especially as a story that shows that we are favoured by the gods, that **we live a charmed life**, that our luck is still holding, and that our planned progression **is still on track**. Over and over again we find that it is possible for a little while to keep up this sort of interpretation of the way our lives are going, but sooner or later something is bound to happen that pricks the bubble. We feel disappointed: why is life against us? Answer: it isn't. It has no settled policies, either of favour or of disfavour. Our mistake was the old one of imagining that the nature of things has a special interest in either raising or humbling us.

Sartre nicely describes the way we see, or constantly try to see, the world in terms of narrative patterns.

> A man is always a teller of tales, he lives surrounded by
> his stories and the stories of others, he sees everything that
> happens to him through them; and he tries to live his life
> as if he were recounting it.[1]

That is true: *sotto voce*, we mutter a running commentary on events all the time, interpreting them in such a way as to keep up our own morale — that is, our confidence in our own myths about ourselves. When we run into fierce opposition and criticism, we have to work particularly hard at maintaining our own self-image; and things are made even more difficult if we rely for support upon ideas of supernatural protection, destiny, and the like. Sooner or later, all the myths are sure to be falsified by events. Life doesn't really have *any* favourites, and we would do better if we learned simply to accept its ups and downs with good humour and no complaints.

This is not an easy lesson to learn. Much more common is the Woody Allen note of wry, self-mocking disappointment:

> 'The food in this place is really terrible.'
> 'Yes, and such small portions.'
> 'That's essentially how I feel about life.'[2]

Before we found ourselves hurled into life we were not given any proper preparation or warnings, so we constantly get nasty surprises: 'Life is not having been told that the man has just waxed the floor.'[3] 'Life is not a spectacle or a feast; it is a predicament.'[4] George Santayana, from whom that last line comes, remarks that everything depends upon whether we can give up the old 'religious' illusion that life, despite appearances, is friendly to us deep down, and learn instead to be content to love life just as it is, with all its uncertainties — and be happy. This is the higher sort of religion which Santayana, I think rightly, sees in Spinoza. As he puts it:

> The truth is cruel, but it can be loved: and it makes free
> those who have loved it.[5]

That is good. If I may be autobiographical, it is a lesson that I was first taught in my teens by studying zoology at school and university, and by being keen on natural history. I was of a generation that took for granted not only Darwinism, but also the new study of animal behaviour that was being inaugurated by people like Otto von Frisch, Konrad Lorenz, David Lack, and N. Tinbergen. Someone who loved the world of living things also had to accept the new recognition of the pitiless harshness of animal life. Without necessarily getting too Nietzschean about it, the extreme beauty and the equally extreme cruelty are part of a single indivisible package and have to be accepted together. One should rejoice in life whilst one can, and one should die without complaint when one must. That is the strange new way of tackling what is usually termed the problem of evil: accept and endure it all, without a murmur of complaint. We overcome evil when we do not let it drive us into bitterness or resentment; the true conquest of evil is simply magnanimity.

Many people will be highly suspicious of what has just been said, taking it as an endorsement of Nietzsche's rejection of pity. That is not so, for in fact I strongly support humanitarianism in social ethics. I reject the ever popular disciplinary moralities of repression and control that seek to use the moral law to restrain the supposed anarchic violence of human nature. I seek instead to base social ethics upon nothing but the affirmation of human solidarity, and pity for human weakness. The phrase that epitomizes this approach to ethics is *the milk of human kindness* — 'kindness' meaning akin-ness. But we'll get a humanitarian ethic right only if we have first accepted **the facts of life**. That means facing up to 'metaphysical evil', our permanent and incurable state of exposure to contingency, finitude and death. We have no right to expect cosmic protection: nothing can really 'cover' us against the possibility of personal disaster at any moment. **That's life**, as the phrase goes: **life's like that, that's the way it goes**, life's chronic insecurity and uncertainty simply have to be accepted. And when we have simply accepted the **facts of life**, *then* we are in a position to talk of **loving life** and of loving our fellow humans.

The Sanctity of Human Life

We have mentioned before a very important feature of Latin Christianity that has for centuries been the key to its history, namely the way in which it institutionalized the classic distinction between sacred and profane realms, developing it into the gulf between two distinct social worlds: the celibate, Latin-speaking and socially-privileged sacred world of the Church – that is, 'the religious life', and the lay, vernacular world of ordinary life and civil society. The sharp distinction between Nature and Grace, or natural and supernatural orders, ran through the whole of theology, and when it was socially institutionalized it easily and deservedly drew fierce criticism.

For example, the Church had its own legal system, and succeeded in winning for 'ecclesiastical persons' (roughly, the clergy and nuns) exemption from proceedings in the civil courts. This privilege, 'benefit of clergy', lasted until 1827 in England, and the clerical thinking associated with it lingers yet in many countries – especially where a bishop treats a serious sexual lapse by a priest not as a civil crime that must be promptly reported to the police, but merely as an offence against ecclesiastical discipline that is to be dealt with internally, and without any publicity. It is not surprising that modern lay people have been outraged to discover that Roman Catholic and Anglican bishops have long been treating the sexual abuse of children by priests in this way, giving little or no thought to the damage done to the victims, who as lay persons belonged to an entirely different jurisdiction.

That is one way the institutionalization of a sharp sacred/secular distinction could lead to scandal and protest. Another way trouble could break out was by lay protest against the Church's habitual devaluation of the whole secular sphere of life. Thus it was (and technically, perhaps, still is) orthodox Christian teaching that the celibate, 'religious' way of life was more perfect than married life in 'the world'. It is not surprising that by the end of the Middle Ages many lay people in the towns – people whose main effort in life had been put into establishing a marriage and a household and raising within it a family of children – were impatient about having their way of life belittled by idle celibates. It is also notable that in late medieval Latin Europe, as in other developed religious civilizations, the bulk of society's entire economic surplus was being spent through religious institutions. The Church, the resources it commanded and the slice of people's lives that it took up, filled up most of the space that is nowadays occupied by education, research, culture, art and entertainment. It is not surprising that by the end of the Middle Ages the whole lay sphere of life was urgently demanding more avenues by which to express itself – and above all, to assert its own *value*.

The process by which all this duly happened is very familiar. For example, the rediscovery of classical antiquity – its literature, its architecture, and its mythology – helped to provide materials for the new secular art and education. The great popularity of poetry and of the theatre provided space in which a new secular selfhood could find a voice, and try itself out in public. And so on. But what we should particularly note here is a transfer of the language of *sanctity* and *inviolability* away from their standard ecclesiastical uses into new lay contexts. The key terms are *holy, sacred, sanctity, sanctuary, sanctum, sacrosanct* and *inviolable / inviolate*. Other terms worth mentioning include *respect, contamination* and *pollution*.

These words are associated with a well known religious phenomenon: like the Queen today, a god needs personal space and may not be approached and physically touched (unless in the former case she initiates the contact, for example in the form of a handshake). In fact, the god's holiness is positively *dangerous*. So his presence or image sits, surrounded by his personal space, in a fenced-off *sanctuary* or *sanctum sanctorum* which only ecclesiastical persons can safely enter. The fence is called a fane, and the area outside it is called profane. In a Western church the symbolic presence of God above the high altar is separated from the public space of the street outside by a whole series of fenced and gated spaces that form an ascending hierarchy of degrees of holiness: the lych-gate gives entrance to the churchyard, the west door to the porch or vestibule of the church building, another gated screen may then give access to the nave, and then the rood screen to the chancel, and the gated communion rail to the sanctuary. There may then be yet more degrees, if the divine presence is seen as being focussed in one or more consecrated eucharistic breads. But we need not take the point any further, for the crucial thing that happened between the Middle Ages and fully developed modernity was that much of this way of thinking and of the language associated with it has been transferred from God to the individual human being. In Christendom, the language of sanctity and inviolability was used to protect the sacred sphere from lay intrusion; now in modernity it begins to be used to protect the freedom and dignity of the lay self.

This can happen in different ways. For example, one who has an audience with the Queen or the Pope may be conducted through a series of chambers, each with a doorkeeper, that lead to the presence chamber – for royal humans are treated rather like gods. But so also can each of us treat his inner self. Because in many religions the god is said to *indwell* the believer, the devotee who practises recollection and introvertive mysticism may similarly see herself as passing through a series of *inner* chambers in order to reach the god within the self, at the heart of the 'interior castle' within each human subject. In addition, religions that recognize the possibility of an incarnation of the divine in a human being offer a third route by which religious language may be transferred from the gods to us humans.

Historically, in the West, the key factor has been space. Mediaeval life was very crowded, and short of becoming a Carthusian, nearly everyone lacked any real privacy, or subjective consciousness, or personal space. However, the later Middle Ages saw a growing demand for subjective consciousness, for personal space, for privacy, for personalized forms of devotion, and ultimately for religious freedom and for human rights; and this has been getting stronger and stronger ever since. Gradually, people won separate bedrooms, single beds, and even their own bathrooms. From childhood, we like to establish and claim some private space, and we try to guard it jealously. Average household size has been getting smaller and smaller for centuries. In this context, the borrowing of religious vocabulary is part of a larger process by which the status of the self is gradually raised.

These familiar changes are reflected in the linguistic shifts that have given us such expressions as the following:

> *My mind is my church* (Tom Paine)
> **The sanctity of marriage**
> **A bird sanctuary**
> **He retired to his sanctum** (= study)
> **The sanctity of the home / of human life / of private life / of human rights**
> *The holiness of the heart's affections* (John Keats)
> **All life is sacred**

Our language has become full of idioms like these: they show us trying to hallow the everyday world – and especially the self, domestic life, and nature. And a good thing too, one may say; but there are at least two major snags. One is that the new usages confuse traditional theology, and have in the long run caused it to disintegrate, and the other is that (especially in the Protestant and Anglo-Saxon cultures) we may have been led to *over*-value private and domestic life, and to *under*-value economic and political life.

This latter failure is perhaps part of the reason for the disappointing results so far of the attempt to invest ordinary lives with epic religious dignity. The seventeenth-century pioneers dreamt of a world in which everyone would live pretty much the same way of life, and all lives would be roughly equal in moral worth. There would be no covetousness, nor envy. Religious societies, colonies and brotherhoods were established in order to realise the ideal, but where are we today? Surrounded by a world that combines a foolish and inflated 'celebrity culture' with an aggressively loutish and self-despising 'street-corner culture'. Why? How could it all have gone so badly wrong?

My argument has been that we have still not yet consistently put life – and in particular, *ordinary* life – first. We need to do this, and then to rethink religion and morality accordingly. We need to get rid of the institutional and psychological relics of an older and now harmful world view, so that in more ways than one we can **come back to life**.

List of Life-Idioms

In a story called 'Rallying Round Old George', Bertie Wooster reports that

> I spent the afternoon musing on Life. If you come to think of it, what a queer thing Life is! So unlike anything else, don't you know, if you see what I mean.

The story is to be found in *My Man Jeeves*, and that is about as far as Bertie Wooster's investigations of the Meaning of Life ever take him. But in literature life-talk crops up all over the place nowadays. In Russell Hoban's new novel *The Bat Tattoo* there is a character who reads Psalm 137: 'How shall we sing the Lord's song in a strange land?', and says unexpectedly, 'Really, that's what life is, isn't it: a strange land?' The phrase becomes something like a motto for the book.

Well, it may be felicitous, but this list does not contain quotations like that one. It contains *only* familiar and readily recognizable life-idioms from everyday speech that are of some general philosophical, religious or ethical interest. I have compiled it from the list given earlier in *The New Religion of Life* (1999), plus additional idioms used in **bold-face Roman** in the text of this book, plus a variety of interesting items pointed out to me by readers. I have also consulted the very useful *New Oxford Dictionary of English* (1998) and a collection of dictionaries of slang, idioms, proverbs and quotations.

The list in *The New Religion of Life* concentrated especially on the strikingly-religious idioms that have entered the language and have become very common within the last 40-50 years. The present expanded list ranges rather more widely. In the process the number of items has risen from about 150 to about 250.

A

Life-affirming (from Nietzsche)
An aim in life
What life is all about
An answer to life's riddle
Appetite for life
Art is long and life is short / *Ars longa vita brevis*
Art of living
Attachment to life
You've got entirely the wrong attitude to life

B

We believe in life before death
The best things in life are free
A blasphemy against life
Bring to life

C

The call of life
A Celebration of the life of …
Facing up to life's challenges
Life changes, and I want to be able to change with it
A charmed life
Life class (life means 'the original': cf. 'large as life')
Clinging to life
Life coach
Take life as it comes
Coming to life
Commitment to life
The right to control my own life
(but) We don't control life
A crime against life
Cultural life
The human life-cycle

D

Live dangerously (Nietzsche)
The dark side/face of life
For dear life
A matter of life and death (film title, 1958)
To deny life
Despair of life

Distrust of life
Drawing from life
Life is not a dress-rehearsal
Domestic life, the sanctity of: see also
Public life, private life, sex life, religious life,
a double life, interior life, etc.

E

Living on the edge (book title)
Life-enhancing (D.H. Lawrence)
Enjoy life
Life is everything
Pronouncing life extinct

F

The facts of life (first used by advocates of sex education)
Life is not fair
Have faith in life
Faithful to life
Life in the fast lane
Fear of life
Feeling more alive / What makes me feel most alive
Fighting for life / to save someone's life
A flicker of life
Something to live for
Life-force (from c.1900: biological vitalism)
Frighten the life out of me
Live fast, die young
Live life to the full / A full life
Full of life
The futility of life

G

Get a life! (c.1989, U.S.A.)
Getting more out of life
Getting on in life
We want to get on with our lives
The gift of life / Take life as a gift
All life belongs to God
Grateful to life / Gratitude for life
Life is the greatest gift of all
Life goes on / Life must go on
My life isn't going anywhere

Life's been good to me / Life's good /
Good living
The good things of/in life

H

.I take my life in my hands
A hard life
Life's hard
Life's been hard on him
He's made life hard for himself
Live hard!
The holiness of life
Where there's life there's hope

I

I've had my life
In love with life
Life on the instalment plan

J

The joy of life, the joy of living
That's nobody's fault, it's just life
There's no justice in life

K

The kiss of life

L

The land of the living (? from N.F.S.
Gruntvig, Denmark)
The lessons of life
A libel on life (Nietzsche)
Life's like that
I want to live my own life
A life to live / Life is for living
Life's a lottery / it's just the luck of
the draw
Life and limb
Live-loving
Lifestyle (c.1973)
Living by the heart (Wordsworth)
To live a lie
I wouldn't be able to live with myself
if ...
Love life while it lasts/while you have
it
The love of life
She loved life

The love of his life
Lust for life
To the life (i.e., just like the original)

M

Life is what you make it
For the life of me
Make the most of life (while you have
it)
The man in your life
What is the meaning of life?
I can't for the life of me ...
In the midst of life (from the Book of
Common Prayer)
The miracle of life/of new life
Don't miss out on life
A mission in life
Surely there's more to life than ...?
Life model
Life must go on
My life! (= my love!)
It's my life/my own life
The mystery of life

N

Nobody is bigger than life
I want to get back to living a normal
life
Not on your life!

O

You only live once
Live life one day at a time
You have one life
We don't own life

P

The pace of life/pulse of life/throb-
bing with life
Life-partner
I feel as if life's passed me by
A passion for life
A path in life/life-path/Walks of life
Perspective upon life
Philosophy of life
Private life
Pro Life (= anti-abortion)
I prefer to remember her as she was in
life

Public life
You need to have a purpose in life
Put some life into it!
You only get out of life what you put into it

Q

Quality of life / Quality-adjusted life-years
Anything for a quiet life
The big questions of life

R

Rage for life
Real life
The religious life
Respect for life / Reverence for life (Albert Schweitzer)
Today is the first day of the rest of your life
The right to life
The life of Reilly/Riley/Larry
You can't run away from life

S

All life is sacred
The sanctity of life
To save lives
She couldn't stop crying to save her life
The secret of life
To see life/to see a bit of life (life = the world)
What life sends
Sex life
Sharing one's life
Life's short/too short
A sin against life
A slice of life
To sort out one's life (c.f. 'life laundry')
That's the story of my life!
The life and soul of the party
Lifespan
A spark of life
The spiritual life
Live never stands still – life moves on
A start in life

Start living
Life-stance (i.e. a faith or philosophy lived-by)
Still life
Stirrings of life
What life has in store for us
That's the story of my life
Struggling for life
Such is life!
Look on the bright side/the sunny side of life
Life is sweet

T

Taking life by the throat
The lesson life has taught me …
Do not tempt life
A Thanksgiving for the Life of …
That's life!
This life / this is the life! / This is your life
I've taken all that life can throw at me
The time of your life
Tired of life
I want to get my life together again
How's life treating you / Is life treating you badly?
Trust in life
True to life / true life

U

Life's apparent unfairness
The university of life (Horatio Bottomley, 1920)
Living life to the utmost
Unworthy to live

V

The value of life
Variety is the spice of life
View of life
A vocation to life

W

Walks of life
Way of life
What I want to do with my own life

Living well
The wheel of life (from Buddhism?)
My life's work
The life-world (E. Husserl)
The worth of life
A life worth living/not worth living
Wrestling with life

Y

Saying Yes to life (Nietzsche)
You've got your whole life before you

Z

Zest for life

It takes time to reconstruct the popular philosophy of life that underlies this body of sayings, and I urge readers to study them carefully. Notice, for example, under the letter C the seemingly paradoxical conjunction of demanding 'the right to control one's own life', whilst also acknowledging that we don't and can't 'control life'. How is this to be explained? In *The New Religion of Life*, chapter 4, I tried to demonstrate in detail how much of our talk about life is closely modelled upon traditional talk about God. In the present book, chapter 9, we see that talk about *my* life, my personal span of life, has recently come to be closely modelled on traditional talk about the soul: I must own it, care for it, accept full responsibility for it, and not 'sell' or betray it, etc. So life in general is rather like God, and *my* life is like my soul – which explains why I say both that I cannot control *life*, and that I have an imperative religious duty to accept responsibility for the control of *my own life*.

Thus great things hang upon small nuances in ordinary language. It seems that we are still so attached to the traditional metaphysics of God and the soul that it enjoys a secular continuation within our talk about life.

Notes

Chapter 1

1 See my *The New Religion of Life in Everyday Speech*. I several times refer to this book in what follows, because I am starting from the data and the argument that it presents – in order this time to turn the argument in a different direction.

2 Here and throughout I follow my earlier practice of printing religiously significant stock phrases about life in **heavy roman** type.

3 *Tractatus Logico–Philosophicus*, 5.621 (Pears and McGuinness translation).

4 *The Discovery of Time* is the title of an interesting book by Stephen Toulmin. *The Discovery of the Mind* is the title of the last major work of the Princeton historian of philosophy Walter Kaufmann. For *bildung*, see for example *Sources of the Self*, by Charles Taylor. On the novelty and innocence of modern urban life, see various of the Impressionist painters, and later, the letters of Van Gogh.

5 On Wordsworth, see my *New Religion of Life*, pp. 25f. The most important mistake in that little book was my failure to recall the Tolstoy quotation. In the L. and A. Maude arrangement of the text of *War and Peace*, it is from Bk 14, chap. 3.

Chapter 2

1 See my *Creation out of Nothing* for an earlier attempt to tackle the same questions. There I drew a contrast between those who pictured the world as having been created once and for all by the language of God, and those who today see us as continually making and remaking our world in and by our own language.

2 The 'envelope' metaphor is from Virginia Woolf's *Mrs Dalloway*; see *The New Religion of Life*, p. 27.

3 On these philosophy of life topics, two short papers of 1915 by Freud deserve mention. They are 'Thoughts for the Times on War and Death', and 'On Transience'. If we find Freud's outlook too pessimistic, we should ask ourselves why we disagree with him. To my mind, he was of a culture that was too hard–driving and disciplinarian, and neglected to cultivate the senses and what Wordsworth calls 'the pleasure which there is in life itself'. Freud himself located the sources of our supposedly chronic and unavoidable unhappiness in the unconscious, but I'd argue that the problem was cultural, and therefore curable. On the question of the value of transient things, of course I agree with him entirely.

4 In the Wallace Collection, London.

Chapter 4

1 English translation by David Bellos, London: Collins/Harvill, 1987.

2 I offer this as an interpretation of what Jean Anouilh means when he says that the job of art is to give life a shape.

3 I take the phrase 'bigger than life' from the film actor Elliott Gould: 'There's a great danger of thinking you're bigger than life. Nobody is bigger than life' — an interesting transfer to life of the traditional warning against hubris. *Daily Telegraph*, 22 March 1999, pp. 14f.

The belief that we can transcend the limitations of our own biological makeup, and live like spirits while still in this life has sometimes been called *angelism*. The implication was clearly that angelism makes a bad mistake: a living human being is always a sexual being, whereas spirits in Christian art always lack secondary sexual characteristics. Angels never have either breasts or beards, and Satan always lacks genitals. Though all this is clear enough, Christian culture usually failed to draw the obvious conclusion: that the very notion that we can and should spend our life preparing for another sexless world 'beyond this life' is badly mistaken. We will never get either religion or morality straight until we admit that we belong here, and only here.

Chapter 5

1 *Deuteronomy* 32:46f.
2 *Deuteronomy* 30:20.
3 *Genesis* 24:2.

Chapter 6

1 In response to my invitation in *The New Religion of Life in Everyday Speech* p. 89.
2 See my *The Meaning of It All in Everyday Speech*.
3 Amongst Christian writers Eckhart is the one who most strongly emphasises – and even conflates — life's gratuitousness and God's grace. See my *Mysticism After Modernity*, pp. 98ff. It is worth recalling that in Christian thought God's creation of the world was not necessitated, but was purely voluntary and *ex nihilo*. Everything therefore is contingent: everything is an effect of grace. What is amusing about Eckhart is the levity with which he can skip from orthodox theistic metaphysics to the view I am putting forward here.

Chapter 7

1 Richard R. Bretell and Joachim Pissarro, *The Impressionist and the City.*
2 *The Impressionist and the City*, p. xxiv, referring to ill. 41.
3 Søren Kierkegaard, for example, was an intensely urban man, who yet could not prevent himself from eyeing the emergent nineteenth-century city with a good deal of the old suspicion. See George Pattison, *'Poor Paris!'*. For Kierkegaard (inevitably) the city is all outward show and no inwardness.

Chapter 8

1 On this whole topic, see Maurice Bloch, *Prey into Hunter*

Chapter 9

1 "Every man is the builder of a temple, called his body, to the god he worships, after a style purely his own, nor can he get off by hammering marble instead. We are all sculptors and painters, and our material is our own flesh and blood and bones. Any nobleness begins at once to refine a man's features, any meanness or sensuality to imbrute them." (Thoreau, *Walden*: penultimate paragraph of ch. XI, "Higher Laws")

Chapter 10

1 See chaps 1 and 4 above. Iris Murdoch uses the sentence: 'Life has no outside' somewhere in *The Philosopher's Pupil*.

2 Maitreya, the plump, laughing Buddha to come, is a good symbol of this. Buddhism is not so life–denying as many have supposed it to be.

3 See for example the creation myths of ancient Egypt and Mesopotamia.

4 See my 'Is Anything Sacred? Christian Humanism and Christian Nihilism', in *Is Nothing Sacred?*, pp. 63–75.

5 This saying is attributed to the broadcaster Chris Evans.

Chapter 11

1 *Persuasion*, 1818, chap.1.

Chapter 12

1 They also say **It's not fair** – the word 'it', like 'things' being often used to signify everything we are up against, the impersonal backdrop or context surrounding our lives. See my *The Meaning of It All in Everyday Speech*.

2 For example, Bernard Williams, *Ethics and the Limits of Philosophy*, London: Collins, 1985, especially chap. 10; John D. Caputo, *Against Ethics*, Bloomington and Indianapolis: Indiana University Press, 1993.

Chapter 14

1 Arthur Schopenhauer, *The World as Will and as Representation*, Third Edition 1859, *Supplements to the Fourth Book*, especially XLVI, 'On the Vanity and Suffering of Life', etc., etc.; and for James on optimism and pessimism, see William James, *The Will to Believe and Other Essays in Popular Philosophy*, 1896, the first three essays, pp. 1–110.

2 J.-J. Rousseau, *Emile*, 1762; Friedrich Schiller, *Letters on the Aesthetic Education of Man*, 1793; standard edition revised by the author, 1801.

3 Michel Foucault, *Le Souci de Soi*, Paris: Gallimard, 1984; ET as *The History of Sexuality, Volume Three: The Care of the Self*.

Chapter 15

1 Jane Austen, *Emma*, 1816.

2 Cited above, chap.1, note 3.

Chapter 17

On stories, see my *What is a Story?*, and two unpublished lectures, 'Journeys, Stories and the Meaning of Life', *Sea of Faith* 14, 2001; and 'Fairytales, Religion and Life', *Sea of Faith* 15, 2002.

Chapter 18

1 See Charles Hartshorne, 'Time, Death and Everlasting Life', in *The Logic of Perfection*,; discussed, with bibliographical notes, in John Hick, *Death and Eternal Life*. 'Recapitulation' theories of immortality, according to which we will live eternally in God's memory or in God's knowledge, are hinted at by various idealist and Whiteheadian philosophers, and from them have spread to certain scientist–theologians who dream that we may enjoy a virtual immortality in the computers of the far future. See Frank J. Tipler, *The Physics of Immortality*, and the earlier, much discussed joint work by John Barrow and F.J. Tipler, *The Anthropic Principle*.

2 E.g., John B. Baillie, *And The Life Everlasting*.

3 Michel Nedo edited the major edition of Wittgenstein's complete literary remains from a small room in Trinity College, Cambridge.

4 The first statement was in *Only Human*, and the most recent is in *Emptiness and Brightness*.

Chapter 19

1 E.g., Aristotle, *Nicomachean Ethics*, 1095a. 19.

Chapter 20

1 'Adonais' (1821).

Chapter 21

1 A mass noun, as opposed to a count noun, is a word like 'luggage' or 'sand': it has no plural and signifies something that cannot be counted.

2 *The Imitation of Christ* (before 1427), I, i. Trans. Betty I. Knott for the Collins Fontana edition of 1963, often reprinted.

3 *Ibid.*

4 *Ibid.*, III. xx.

5 *Ibid.*, I. xxii.

Chapter 22

1 London: SCM Press, 1999.

2 The website from which he sent me extensive printouts is called COBUILDirect. It offers language data based on the Bank of English corpus of modern spoken and written English.

3 Newspaper interview, *The Daily Telegraph*, 22 March 1999, pp. 14f.

4 Purchased at Kettle's Yard, Cambridge. Could it be by Gillian Wearing? She also contributes a poster that says EVERYTHING IS CONNECTED IN LIFE / THE POINT IS TO KNOW AND UNDERSTAND IT. Very Hegelian.

5 *Luke* 18:1–5.

6 *Friedrich Nietzsche: Selected Letters*, ed. Christopher Middleton, p. 251.

7 *Genesis* 32:22–32.

Chapter 23

1 *The Origin of Species*, 1859 and all later edns., chap. XV 'Recapitulation and Conclusion', *ad fin*.

2 Neal C. Gillespie, *Charles Darwin and the Problem of Creation*, pp. 21ff.

Chapter 24

1 John D. Caputo, *On Religion*.

Chapter 25

1 Emily Brontë, *Wuthering Heights*, 1847, chap. XVI.

Chapter 26

1 *Inferno*, Cant.1.

2 *Exodus* 24:9–11.

3 Thomas Hobbes, *Leviathan*, Part I, chap. 11, the second paragraph.

4 Cited from my *Mysticism After Modernity*, pp. 98–104.

Chapter 27

1 August Weismann, *The Germ-plasm*, 1892, Eng. trans. 1893; G.J. Romanes, *An Examination of Weismannism*, 1902.

2 In Plato's *Phaedo*, Simmias puts forward the comparison of the soul with a candle flame. In Buddhist writings there is a strong interest in freeing us altogether from the notion of an enduring metaphysical soul substance. For example, Buddhaghosa, *Visuddhi Magga*, XVI, 90:

> For there is suffering, but none who suffers;
> Doing exists, although there is no doer;
> Extinction is, but no extinguished person;
> Although there is a path, there is no goer.
> (cited by John Hick, in his *Death and Eternal Life*, London: Collins, 1976.)

Chapter 29

1 Appropriately, I have no reference for it.

2 Schopenhauer himself points out that no philosopher before him was willing to do justice to the importance of sex. See *The World as Will and Representation*, chap. XLIV, 'The Metaphysics of Sexual Love', Vol. II, pp. 532f.

3 From Dylan Thomas, *Under Milk Wood*, 1954.

Chapter 30

1 *A Treatise of Human Nature*, 1739, Bk. II, Part III, Sect. III; Selby–Bigge edition, Oxford: the Clarendon Press, p.415.

Chapter 31

1 From *Nausea*, 1938, Saturday, noon.

2 From the film *Annie Hall*.

3 Ogden Nash, *You and Me and P.B. Shelley*.

4 George Santayana, reference untraced.

5 *Ibid.*, from his Introduction to Spinoza's *Ethics*.

A Note about Books

Dictionaries

I begin with a note about dictionaries, because the student of idioms and stock phrases needs criteria by which to judge how well-established in the language a particular phrase is. We cannot rely only on a personal sense of familiarity; we need also to see a phrase used in the media, and cited in dictionaries.

I use the well-known Oxford dictionaries, including *The Oxford English Dictionary*, Second Edition of 1989, reprinted with corrections, 1991; *The New Oxford Dictionary of English*, ed. Judy Pearsall, 1998; *The Oxford Dictionary of English Idioms*, edd. A.P. Cowie, R. Mackin and I.R. McCaig, 1993; and *The Oxford Concise Dictionary of Proverbs*, edited by John Simpson, 1982, reissued 1996. In addition to the well-known *Oxford Dictionary of Quotations*, I use *The Penguin Dictionary of Modern Quotations*, edd. J.M. and M.J. Cohen, Second Edition, New York: Penguin Books, 1980.

Very good evidence of the currency of phrases is the fact that foreigners need to learn them when they are being taught spoken English. TEFL books (Teaching English as a Foreign Language) are very useful, and the big Collins two-language popular dictionaries, English-French/French-English and English-German/ German-English, have particularly full lists of phrases.

The outstanding work on slang is *The Cassell Dictionary of Slang*, ed. Jonathon Green, London: Cassell, 1998. Finally, the student must not forget that nowadays many good new phrases first enter the language as book, film and song titles. Again there are many standard reference works, and I favour *Halliwell's Film and Video Guide*, a new edition of which still comes each year from Harper Collins of London and New York. This class of phrases have the great advantage of coming each with a date attached. At least one is entitled to conclude that the phrase was already current at the time, or became current from the time, that the title was issued or published. So dated titles give a little help with the often-difficult question of dating generally.

In general, I must insist that the 'ordinary-language' or 'democratic' theology and philosophy that I am trying to write cannot succeed unless we are as rigorous as the best journalists with our criteria for identifying phrases, dating them, and establishing their currency.

Other Modern Works Referred To

Baillie, John B. *And The Life Everlasting*. New York: Scribners, 1933.
Barrow, John D., and Tipler, Frank J. *The Anthropic Principle*. 1986.

Bloch, Maurice. *Prey into Hunter* (Lewis Henry Morgan Lectures at the University of Rochester, 1981). Cambridge, England: Cambridge University Press, 1992.

Bretell, Richard R. and Pissarro, Joachim. *The Impressionist and the City: Pissarro's Series Paintings.* Yale University Press, for Dallas Museum of Art, Philadelphia Museum of Art and London Royal Academy of Arts, 1992.

Caputo, John D. *Against Ethics.* Bloomington and Indianapolis: Indiana University Press, 1993.

____ *On Religion.* London and New York: Routledge (Thinking in Action Series), 2001.

Cupitt, Don. *Only Human.* London: SCM Press, 1985.

____ *What is a Story?* London: SCM Press, 1991.

____ *Creation out of Nothing.* London: SCM Press and Philadelphia: Trinity Press International, 1990.

____ *The New Religion of Life in Everyday Speech.* London: SCM Press, 1999.

____ *The Meaning of It All in Everyday Speech.* London: SCM Press, 1999.

____ *Kingdom Come in Everyday Speech.* London: SCM Press, 2000.

____ *Mysticism After Modernity.* Oxford and Malden, MA: Blackwell, 1998.

____ *Is Nothing Sacred? The Non-Realist Philosophy of Religion: Selected Essays.* New York: Fordham University Press, 2002.

Foucault, Michel. *The History of Sexuality, Volume Three: The Care of the Self.* New York: Random House, 1986.

Freud, Sigmund, 'Thoughts for the Times on War and Death', 1915; in *Collected Papers, Volume IV*, no. XVII. London: The Hogarth Press, 1956.

____ 'On Transience', 1915; in *Collected Papers, Volume V*, no. VII. London: The Hogarth Press, 1957.

Gillespie, Neal C. *Charles Darwin and the Problem of Creation.* Chicago: Chicago University Press, 1979.

Hartshorne, Charles. *The Logic of Perfection.* La Salle, IL: Open Court, 1962.

Hick, John. *Death and Eternal Life.* London: Collins, 1976.

Middleton, Christopher, ed. *Friedrich Nietzsche: Selected Letters.* Chicago: Chicago University Press, 1969.

Pattison, George. *'Poor Paris!': Kierkegaard's Critique of the Spectacular City.* Kierkegaard Studies, Monograph Series 2. Berlin and New York: Walter de Gruyter, 1999.

Perec, Georges. *Life: A User's Manual.* Translated by David Bellos. London: Collins/ Harvill, 1987.

Schopenhauer, Arthur. *The World as Will and Representation*, Third Edition. Translated by E.F.J. Payne, in two volumes. New York: Dover Books, 1969.

Taylor, Charles. *Sources of the Self: The Making of the Modern Identity.* Cambridge, England: Cambridge University Press, 1989.

Tipler, Frank J. *The Physics of Immortality: Modern Cosmology, God and the Resurrection of the Dead.* London and New York: Macmillan, 1994.

Toulmin, Stephen. *The Discovery of Time.* London: Hutchinson, 1965.

Williams, Bernard. *Ethics and the Limits of Philosophy.* London: Collins, 1985.

Wittgenstein, Ludwig. *Tractatus Logico-Philosophicus.* Translated by D.F. Pears and B.F. McGuinness. London: Routledge and Kegan Paul, 1974.

Index